PARENTS and PROTECTORS

A STUDY IN CHILD ABUSE AND NEGLECT

DEBORAH SHAPIRO

RESEARCH CENTER

CHILD WELFARE LEAGUE OF AMERICA, INC.
67 Irving Place, New York, N.Y. 10003

CHILD WELFARE LEAGUE OF AMERICA

67 Irving Place, New York, New York 10003

Library of Congress Catalog Card Number: 79-88223

ISBN: 0-87868-139-6

Current printing (last digit)
10 9 8 7 6 5 4 3 2 1

PRINTED IN THE UNITED STATES OF AMERICA

For Geraldine Simpson,
the most conscientious of
colleagues

TABLE OF CONTENTS

FOREWORD

Protective service--service in the interests of children who are neglected or abused--is crucial to the well-being of a very large number of children. In 1961 neglect, abuse or exploitation by parents or others responsible for the child's care was the principal problem of 36% of the 377,000 children served by public child welfare agencies.[1] In 1977 the same problem ranked first among the reasons for service to the 1.8 million children who received service from public departments providing social services to children and their families.[2]

Protective services of adequate quantity and quality have long been a primary concern of the Child Welfare League of America. The League took leadership in pressing for provision of such services by public agencies throughout the country to ensure universal availability. And it issued standards for protective service as a guide and a goal for agencies and communities in developing services of good quality.[3] The Standards are, however, based on the best judgment of an interdisciplinary group of experts, not on empirical data. What kind of service works with whom has been a major preoccupation of the League's Research Center, but it had not hitherto undertaken a study of protective service, as such.

As Dr. Shapiro points out in the last chapter of this report, public interest in protective service has been aroused only over the last decade or so when instances of gross physical abuse of children have received attention in the popular press. The much more common but less dramatic problem of neglect, which may have equally devastating effects on children, has not captured the public imagination. In fact, it has not attracted comparable attention on the part of professionals. The League considers it of utmost importance that problems of neglect and its treatment be accorded serious attention.

The League welcomed passage of the Child Abuse Prevention and Treatment Act of 1974, which authorized establishment of the National Center on Child Abuse and Neglect (NCCAN), whose title does include the word "neglect," conspicuously missing from the title of the Act. The League also welcomed the announcement of the availability of grants for research on various aspects of child abuse and neglect.

In 1974 CWLA applied for a grant to study the factors operating to reduce abusive and neglectful behavior, or, as we interpreted it, to examine the effectiveness of protective service. Our initial intent was to study families participating in Parents Anonymous as well as families served by official agencies, but NCAAN discouraged this for reasons of no interest here, and our proposal focused on families who had received service from public child welfare agencies because of abuse or neglect of children.

It was our good fortune that Deborah Shapiro was on the League's research staff at the time our application was written. Not only did we have the benefit of her participation in developing the research proposal, but we had an ideal project director immediately available when we were notified in the spring of 1975 that our application had been approved and funded. Because of the uncertainties of funding, it is all too common that a project director has to be recruited to carry out a research plan developed entirely by someone else.

Dr. Shapiro was an ideal person to direct this project, not only because of her long experience in child welfare research, but because of her high level of frustration tolerance. For this was a singularly frustrating study. Since funding was available for only 2 years, the only practical way that we could see to look at the effects of service was through a retrospective study directed to families served 2 or 3 years earlier. This design created severe problems for the research staff and for the participating agencies in sample selection, in locating and obtaining participation of elegible families, and in identifying changes in functioning in the families in the absence of baseline data about them. Probably the strongest conclusion to be drawn from this research is that the effectiveness of service can be examined definitively only if cases for study are selected at point of intake and followed systematically thereafter.

Another frustrating experience, but one from which useful information emerged, was the drastic shrinkage of the numbers of elegible cases anticipated by the participating agencies. From agency data it appeared that it would be easy to obtain 250 cases from five agencies. In fact, only 171 cases were secured despite the addition of a sixth agency. Part of the shrinkage resulted from inability to reach eligible families, but a larger part was due to the considerable proportion of the cases referred to the agencies for protective service in which neither abuse nor neglect was identified, but to which the agencies provided supportive service to avert such problems. It is good to know that preventive service is being provided to a substantial number of families and that the incidence of abuse and neglect is lower than protective agency caseloads suggest, but nonabusive, non-neglectful families hardly fit this study of lessening of abusive or neglectful behavior.

The findings of the study that a considerable majority of the families showed some improvement in childrearing and had a positive attitude toward the agency and its services are encouraging. But we are left with a nagging feeling that the inevitable self-selection of study participants may have weighted the sample with more successful cases.

That improvement cannot be effected quickly or easily in disadvantaged families with multiple problems has been indicated in other League studies.[4] Here too we find improvement more likely in cases served for at least 2 years and receiving several practical services as well as counseling.

As to which families are likely to benefit, the findings are thin. Younger mothers with good housekeeping practices and nonauthoritarian attitudes showed better outcomes than others. No other characatersitic differentiated cases by level of improvement. Again in a prospective study with solid baseline data it might be possible to identify additional family characteristics and circumstances associated with successful outcome. However, under the best conditions, it is very difficult to unravel the combination of features in family, situtation and service that "work." The difficulty of the problem should not lead to the conclusion that it is hopeless, but to recognition that its solution requires a great deal of time, effort and patience. As Dr. Shapiro points out, we still lack both a typology of child maltreatment that satisfactorily differentiates various forms of neglect and abuse and adequate means of measuring improvement in family functioning.

In the meantime, this research contributes several more pieces to the puzzle of the factors in neglect and abuse and their treatment.

Ann W. Shyne
CWLA Research Director 1968-76

1. Jeter, Helen R., Children, Problems and Services in Child Welfare Programs, Children's Bureau, 1963, p. 2.

2. Public Social Services for Children and Their Families, Children's Bureau, in press.

3. CWLA Standards for Child Protective Service, revised 1973.

4. For example, Sherman, Edmund A., et al. Services to Children in Their Own Homes, CWLA, 1970, and Jones, Mary Ann, et al. A Second Chance for Families, CWLA, 1976.

ACKNOWLEDGMENTS

This study, like all others, is the collaborative product of the research staff who plan, collect, analyze, and report the data provided, made available only through the cooperation of clients and agency staff. We are indebted to the following agencies and their staff for their efforts in behalf of this study.

Agency	Liaison/Coordinator	Interviewers
Westchester County Dept. of Welfare White Plains, NY	David Honings Margaret McDaniel	Ann Aukamp Brett Ayvazian Nancy Bave Joy de Luna
Denver Dept. of Social Services Denver, CO	Ruth Reynolds William Lindsey	Frederick Acosta Joseph Bagan Lynn Clark Helen Petersen Jeannine Williamson
Montgomery County Children's Services Bs. Dayton, OH	Alberta Lewis Diane Brads Lenore Adams	Janet Jackson Sharon Jones Charlotte Lemming Cheryl Turner
Hennepin County Dept. of Welfare Minneapolis, MN	Philip Dolinger Roger Joing	Roger Joing Nancy Baltins Nicky Bredeson
Trumbull County Children's Services Bd. Warren, OH	Craig Neuman Joseph White, Jr.	Sheryl Kinsley Jerry Muzyka Emma Rivers Vincent Stigliano

Knox County Dept. of   Mary Lou Chambers   Elizabeth Ganoe
Human Services   Diana Edmondson   Deborah Painter
Knoxville, TN   Karen Stephens
                                                        Dorothy Strange
                                                        Margaret Thomas

For the League staff, my indebtedness to Geraldine Simpson, Research Associate for the study, who supervised data collection and coding, and carried out the analysis, is expressed in the dedication of this report to her. She was ably assisted by Alan Reich and Thelma Barry, who had the difficult task of coding complex data. Anne moore, our departmental secretary, assisted in the coding and then typed the manuscript with her usual high level of accuracy. Karen Brown, who preceded her in that position, handled the project's correspondence and reports to the funding agency and preliminary drafts of the first chapters.

Ann Shyne, who was director of research at the time the study was funded, wrote the proposal and provided support that contributed amply to the maintenance of the high level of frustration tolerance with which she credits me in her forword.

Joseph H. Reid, now retired as executive director of the League, provided support and guidance on some of the more intricate problems of budget and staff management. More important, Mr. Reid is one of the few executives in the social welfare field who can be credited with 22 years of consistent support for a field-oriented research program in his agency.

Mrs. Cecelia Sudia, our project officer from the Office of Child Development, now the Administration for Children, Youth and Families, was an unfailing source of support and encouragement as she always is. In this instance, I am particularly appreciative of the constant supply of interim and prepublication reports made available to us without which most of the last chapter could not have been written.

Finally, on behalf of the Child Welfare League, appreciation is expressed for the funding of the study by the National Center on Child

Abuse and Neglect, Children's Bureau, Administration on Children, Youth and Families, Office of Human Development Services, U.S. Department of Health, Education and Welfare, Grant #90-C-429.

Deborah Shapiro, D.S.W.
Director of Research

Chapter I
DESIGN OF THE STUDY

The Child Abuse Prevention and Treatment Act of 1974 marked the first major federal intervention in a social problem that has been a growing source of concern, at least since the early 1960s, a concern that shows no sign of declining in the 1970s. Once considered a rare form of pathology, viewed with disbelief and denial by the general public and by professionals, child abuse and child neglect have become the subject of mandatory reporting in every state. Increases in reporting, together with the attention paid by the media to extreme cases, resulted in continuous pressure for action, culminating in the passage of the 1974 Act. It authorized the establishment of the National Center on Child Abuse and Neglect, empowering the Center to make grants or enter into contracts with public and voluntary agencies for demonstration projects and to conduct research. The Center then identified a series of issues for which it solicited research proposals. These issues included questions about the causes and precipitating factors involved in abuse and neglect, the effects on children, and the cost-effectiveness of services. The Research Center of the Child Welfare League successfully submitted a proposal that responded to one of these questions: "What are the operative factors or pervasive influences that result in the permanent discontinuation of abusive or neglectful behavior in some parent figures and recidivism in others?"

In the course of planning the study, the term "permanent" was dropped in recognition of the fact that the 2-year maximum permitted by the funding agency prohibited a longitudinal design that would have been necessary to assess the durability of any change in behavior. It was recognized that a single cycle of data collection involving information given retrospectively would create many analytic problems, but the importance of the subject encouraged a decision in favor of using the opportunity for the knowledge it might yield for further research. The objective of the study was, as stated in the proposal, "to identify the factors in services provided and in the family's life situation that are associated with, and presumably effective in, discontinuation of abusive or neglectful behavior on the part of parental figures, and the circumstances under which these factors are and are not effective."

As would be expected with a problem of increasing general concern, the literature on the subject is massive and continuously expanding. With relatively few exceptions, however, it has tended to focus heavily on descriptive material, usually based on clinical experience. Professionals from several disciplines have written and continue to write about the family background and characteristics of abusive and neglectful parents, their expectations of their children, the motivation for their behavior, and the circumstances that are likely to predict incidents of abuse. A smaller body of literature describes the problems of protective services programs directed to the identification and treatment of cases of abuse and neglect. Relatively little attention has been given to the effectiveness of these programs in modifying the behavior of parents or to the individual, family, and environmental circumstances associated with such modifications. The general picture created by the clinical literature is that of parents who are socially isolated, inaccessible or not readily accessible to professional help, and who require considerable patient effort on the part of professional helpers over long periods of time. Young's study showed that neglectful parents were somewhat more likely to change their behavior than abusers.[1] Apart from this, the literature offered virtually no leads or clues either as to factors that might distinguish a parent who is receptive to change from one unlikely to change, or as to what factors in service programs are more likely to bring about change than others. Kadushin notes that, as of 1974, there were no well designed evaluation studies to establish the exact degree of success achieved by protective services. He describes a number of practice studies reporting success rates ranging from 30% to 75%.[2] None of these gave any indication of factors in the treatment situation associated with different degrees of

Much of what is written about treatment, both traditional and innovative, implies that duration and intensity of service as well as worker skill are associated with change. Various intensive treatment programs have been developed in various locations, usually based in hospitals. Parental self-help groups such as Parents Anonymous have also been developed and promoted, as well as other innovative methods, such as the use of lay therapists. Like most innovations, they receive considerable attention from the media, and enthusiastic claims for success are made by their adherents. Many of these programs are, however, too new and, in many instances, involve too few subjects to permit rigorous assessment.

While this manuscript was in preparation, the Berkeley Planning Associates published its reports on the evaluation of 11 child abuse and neglect demonstration projects. Findings of the Berkeley reports, specifically in the study dealing with impact on adult clients, parallel to findings in this study are discussed in the final chapter of this study. At this point, it is sufficient to note that only 42% of the clients in the Berkeley sample were reported to have a "reduced propensity for future abuse or neglect." A high rate of re-incidence (30%) of abuse or neglect while in treatment was also noted, indicating in the opinion of the authors that the field's current level of knowledge of successful intervention methods is poor.[3] An evaluation of the Parents Anonymous program has also recently been completed by Behavior Associates, Inc. Its findings, in contrast to the Berkeley report indicate a high degree of success, but the evaluative methods used in the two studies differed markedly and questions can be raised as to whether the same population is being served.[4]

The Study Design

The design of this study was diagnostic-descriptive in the Kahn-Finestone classification system.[5] To obtain the information needed to describe the relationship between the dependent variable of reduction of abusive or neglectful behavior and the independent variables describing the parents and the service given, interviews were planned with parents who had been identified as abusive or neglectful by the protective services departments to which complaints had been made. Data from the interviews were to be supplemented by data obtained from case records.

The time period to be covered by each interview was set at approximately 2 to 3 years; complaints, therefore, had to have been initiated in 1972-73. This was recognized as a relatively brief period to observe changes in parental behavior but it was considered to be sufficiently long to reflect effects of service. It also was not so long as to permit service effects to be confounded by long-term community and family developments. A longer time period would have made it more difficult to locate the cases identified for inclusion. The original intent was to collect 100-250 interviews; data collection problems, to be described later, resulted in a final sample of 171.

Cooperating Agencies.[6] Six protective services agencies agreed to cooperate with the project to identify appropriate subjects. The Westchester County Department of Social Services, located in White Plains, New York, north of New York City, contributed 42 cases to the sample. This department serves a population of over 800,000 and has six district offices in communities ranging from 18,000 to 190,000.

Several of these communities have large black populations. Departmental staff estimated that approximately half the population served is black. The department has a 24-hour emergency intake service, and offers counseling, foster care, homemaker service and day care.

The Montgomery County Children Services Board, located in Dayton, Ohio, contributed 30 cases to the sample. It serves a metropolis of over 500,000 and, like Westchester, has a large black community. Staff also estimated that about half the population served is black. In 1974, the department served a total of 1705 children. Of these, 318 were allegedly abused. Its services included counseling, homemakers, an emergency shelter, and foster home placement.

The Trumbull County Children Services Board in Warren, Ohio, contributed 34 Cases. It serves an industrialized county in the northeastern part of the state, with a population of 230,000 divided among five municipalities and 24 townships. The population served is almost entirely white, with a black minority estimated at 6% to 10%. The agency offers a range of services including school social work, homemaker service, foster care, adoption, day care, and residential treatment. In 1973, 130 children for whom the agency took custody were involved in cases of abuse and neglect.

The Hennepin County Department of Welfare in Minneapolis contributed 25 cases. It serves a population of nearly a million, largely white but with black and Indian minorities. As in the other communities, the minorities are over-represented in the service population. The department has a protective services division of 45 workers, divided into five units. A 1973 report indicated that the department served an average of 2100 children and their families each month. In that year, 580 new cases of neglect were reported. These included 168 cases of physical abuse. In 1974, 173 children were reported as physically abused.

The Denver County Social Services Department in Denver, Colorado, contributed 25 cases to the study. This department serves a city and county population of over 500,000. It includes a children and youth services division responsible for child protection. The total population of children served increased from 8231 in 1974 to 9245 in 1977. Of the 777 children seen by protective services, 36% were white, 31% Hispanic and 23% black; the remaining 10% were of other races or unkown. In contrast, the general population of the area is 72% white, 17% Hispanic and 9% black. As with the other agencies, the number of children reported as abused or neglected increases annually. This agency reported 595 cases in 1976 in contrast to 425 in 1975.

Unlike the other agencies, most of the staff involved in this division had master's degrees in social work. Like the other departments, it offers a full range of traditional child welfare services. It also has a family crisis center, a hotline service, parents' aides, and Parents Anonymous groups. These services, however, were introduced after the period covered by the study and had little impact on the sample involved.

The Knox County Department of Human Services serving Knoxville, Tennessee, an urban area with a population of over 250,000, contributed 15 cases. This agency participated on the recommendation of the Tennessee Department of Human Services when it was found necessary to broaden the base for data collection to ensure an adequate sample. The social service division of this department, with a staff of over 100 workers, includes a protective services unit, which takes referrals of abuse or neglect involving families not already known to the agency for other reasons. Thus, workers with general child welfare caseloads serve abuse and neglect cases when the family is on public assistance or known to the agency for some other reason. Since the abuse registry was established the same year the study period began, figures representing change are available for only a 2-year period. State reports indicate that this department served 2016 families in 1973. Of these, 187 were classified as protective service cases. In 1973-74, 321 were so classified, for an increase of 41%. In 1974-75, 395 were so classified, for an increase of 19%. The range of services offered by the department was similar to that of the other agencies.

Sample Selection. The initial plan for this study called for a sample of 250 families, of which the cooperating agencies were to contribute 50 families each. Initially this seemed a reasonable quota since the available statistics for all the agencies suggested a supply of eligible cases more than sufficient to allow for the usual response problems of refusals and geographic mobility. Experience, however, soon indicated that the pool of eligible cases was not as large as was anticipated. Originally, it was expected that all families whose cases were opened in 1973, including cases open earlier, would be eligible except those where contact was minimal (defined as three or fewer contacts with a social worker), those extreme cases where children were immediately and permanently placed with no offer of service to their parents, and those where neither parent was accessible.

To meet the study's goals, the families in the sample had to share two essential characteristics: a substantiated complaint or at least a strong suspicion of neglect or abuse, and an opportunity to respond to an offer of service. Since the study aimed to describe factors associated with the discontinuation of abuse and neglect, there was obviously no point in including families where such behavior was suspected but not proved. At the other extreme, it seemed pointless to include families whose children were removed quickly and where the parents were not given service, since this would be tantamount to "proving" that parents will stop abusing and neglecting children when the latter are taken away. Since the study also proposed to examine the role of service in effecting change, there also seemed no point in including those families whose contact was too limited for any response to be expected. It was also considered necessary to exclude from the study any cases where the parents were not accessible even though the whereabouts of the children and their caretakers were known. Though interviewing an informed relative might have been possible, the firsthand report of an abusing or neglecting parent or spouse seemed an indispensable requirement; secondhand data would have posed too many analytic problems.

Initially, most of the agency staff consulted thought that the exclusion criteria presented few problems. The number of cases or amount of time spent on investigating complaints that proved to be invalid was not considered significant. Staff also maintained that cases of immediate, permanent removal were rare, as were cases involving a relative as substitute parent. The number of cases in which contact might be minimal could not be estimated, but again was considered likely to be low because of the agency's mandate to pursue complaints.

After the initial field visits, however, it became clear that agencies varied somewhat in their definition of eligibility, and that service was often given to families who were not appropriate candidates for the study. In three agencies, services were offered with varying frequency on "preventive" grounds -- that is, abuse or neglect was not actually charged and sometimes not even suspected; the family, however, was considered vulnerable and it was thought best to offer them services rather than refer them elsewhere. Other apparently inappropriate cases involved adolescents beaten by parents for sexual activity or taking drugs. Such cases, which in the past would have been referred to the juvenile justice system, are redefined by the police in some communities as "child abuse" and referred to protective services. One agency accepted such cases on grounds that such actions reflected the community's definition of child abuse. Other agencies thought that these were not the cases for which protective services were intended and referred them elsewhere. Since most of the cases involving adolescents appeared to result in placement in residential treatment where the adolescents, rather than the parents, became the focus of treatment, there seemed to be little point in their inclusion in a study such as this. An additional criterion was therefore introduced, namely, that at least one of the abused or neglected children in the family be under 12 years of age.

8

Another problem of a different order appeared in one agency when it was discovered that the 1973 statistics from the local registry, which provided the basis for estimates of eligible cases, reflected the number of complaints rather than the number of families involved. Since new complaints could be and were made in relation to families active before 1973, the number of cases eligible for the study was smaller than anticipated.

All of these factors meant that the ratio of ineligible to eligible cases in most agencies was not only larger than had been anticipated, but also more staff work was required to identify the eligible families. Since confidentiality requirements precluded case selection by research staff, this process had to be handled by agency personnel with the aid of written instructions and conferences with research staff. One agency dealt with the problem by organizing a "crash" review of 1973 records on a single Saturday with the assistance of all the available staff. The coordinator then telephoned a report to the League office that, of 272 cases reviewed, 197 were ineligible by study criteria. Sixteen families were inaccessible (no current address, left the area). Only 59 were both eligible and apparently accessible, and of this group, only 15 were finally reached.

In addition to the eligibility problems, initial efforts to reach the eligible families resulted in only about four out of 10, at the most, responding directly by returning a signed consent form to the agency. Direct refusals were uncommon; the most typical response was not to answer the letter at all. As one of the interviewers commented after a successful inperson attempt to obtain cooperation, "Protective services clients expect you to come after them." Application was made to the funding agency for a supplemental grant to permit payment to potential respondents at the rate of $20 per family. Agencies were also to be reimbursed for staff time spent in the field, locating clients who did not respond. After payment went into effect, several coordinators reported that the response improved but the impact did not increase the sample to the size originally anticipated. Figures from the agencies indicate, however, that the problem was more that of an unexpectedly high proportion of ineligible families than of client unresponsiveness.

Agency staff were asked to fill out a form for each case reviewed but time pressures and staff shortages made it impossible to do so in all instances. From the four agencies for which figures were obtainable, it was evident that seven cases had to be read for every interview achieved. The overall proportion of ineligible cases was 60% and ranged from a low of 41% in one agency to a high of 72% in another. Twenty-six percent of the total number of cases reviewed were of families who met the study criteria but could not be reached. This proportion ranged from a low of 18% in one agency to a high of 72% in another. Thus in only 14% of all cases reviewed were interviews obtained. The proportion of interviews obtained out of the total number eligible was 35%, ranging from 2% to 55% in the four agencies. As was indicated in the figures given for each agency, none was able to meet the quota of 50 cases, including the largest. Clearly there were far more cases involving unvalidated complaints or brief contacts, more cases served for "preventive" reasons, and more involving children who were all over 12 than either research or agency staff had expected.

Data Collection. Twenty-six interviewers were hired for the study, four each in four agencies and five in each of the remaining two. In light of the difficulites anticipated in reaching the study sample, experienced protective services workers familiar with the areas served by the agency were considered the best candidates for interviewers. All six agencies gave permission for their workers to do work for the study. All but one interviewer averaged 2 to 4 years in protective services; the exception worked in a school unit that handled referrals to protective services. The interviewing staff included seven men. Three of the interviewers were black and one was of Chicano origin. Some matching with respondents by sex and race was possible, although not as much as would have been desirable with the client population at issue. Ten of the interviewers had B.A. degrees, six had bachelor's degrees in social work, eight had M.S.W. degrees, and two had advanced degrees in other fields. Six held supervisory positions in their agencies.

The employment of "moonlighting" workers, not hitherto attempted on any League research project, had the benefit of gaining for the study knowledgeable interviewers who not only did not need orientation to the problem, but contributed to the research staff's understanding and to the development of the instruments used. They were often more motivated than most interviewers by their interest in the results of the study. They remained with the study for the duration of the data collection period, with only one "dropout."

However, the dual role played by the interviewers placed them in a sensitive situation in the agency, since they could obtain information on and evaluate the work of fellow staff members. There was also the possibility of conflict between the research and the service role. These problems were discussed in training sessions. No significant problems arose during the course of data collection, so far as is known to the research staff, perhaps because of the relatively small number of interviews collected in each agency.

Study procedures prohibited the assignment of interviewers to any cases on which they had been active themselves and, whenever possible, assignments were made outside the interviewers' own units. They were also instructed to inform respondents that they were employed as protective services workers and on temporary assignment for the League, to avoid the embarrassment and suspicion that might arise from chance recognition. An interviewers' manual was prepared and potential problems were discussed in training sessions. There was strong consensus among all those concerned that professional discipline was of a sufficiently high caliber to avoid any major problems; subsequent experience showed that this confidence was not misplaced.

Instruments. The major data collection instruments were the parent interview schedule and the case reading schedule. The interview was usually addressed to the mother but provision was made for inclusion of the father when appropriate. Mothers were interviewed alone in 80% of the families, both parents in 12%, and the father only in 8%. The interview covered family composition, the parents' versions of the circumstances of their involvement with protective services, the type of service and the family's reactions to the service. It also included the family's experience with the courts, if any. This was followed by a description of the family's current situation, including their economic status, housing, extended family and social relations. The respondents were asked to give information about each child reared, whether or not he or she was in the home or involved in the abuse/neglect problem. This section covered the child's health, school status, and relations with siblings, peers, significant adults and parents. Toward the end of the interview respondents were asked about their own childhood to elicit information about the extent to which they themselves might have been abused or neglected. At the end of the interview the parent was given a self-administered 25-item question-naire that included three attitude scales, measuring self-esteem, authoritarian childrearing practices, and accessibility to help from social workers. The self-esteem measure consisted of nine of the 10 items in the Rosenberg Self-esteem Scale.[7] The measures of authoritarianism in childrearing were original items developed for the study when a search of the literature indicated that no appropriate measure was available. The items designed to measure accessibility were based in part on items used by the Family Welfare Research Program at the Columbia University School of Social Work.

The parent interview schedule also contained precoded questions that permitted the interviewer to record impressions of the family and, when the case reading was completed, to note any factual discrepancies or differences in impressions. The interviewers were also asked to evaluate the quality of service given.

The case reading schedule called for the family composition as given in the record, a count of worker activities, a precoded description of the complaint and of current living conditions, and a summary of whatever material might have been available in the record about the parents' early history. Case records were read by the interviewer after the interview was completed, with the written permission of the respondent; only one respondent refused to give permission. The schedule also called for a description of the parent's response to the agency worker and to the agency services offered. The list of family stresses that are part of the form used by the National Clearinghouse on Child Abuse and Neglect was introduced into the case reading schedule. In addition, the reader was asked to check all indicators of progress or lack of progress noted in the record. In general, most of the data in the case reading schedule paralleled the data obtained in the interview, to permit comparisons between the parents' own perception of the situation and that of the workers involved.

Since it was anticipated that many of the cases involved would be currently active or recently closed, the worker assigned was asked to review the case reading schedule and add any relevant information that might not have been in the record. If no worker was available, a supervisor's review was accepted. The workers were also asked to fill out short forms giving their evaluation of the client's response, as well as pertinent information about themselves, such as education and experience. The worker's supervisor was also asked to give a brief precoded general evaluation of the worker's performance. This last form was added at the suggestion of one of the agency administrators who, noting the great variability in the quality of casework given in his department, thought that this assessment of worker performance, together with parent attitudes, the interviewer's evaluation, and the worker's assessment of the satisfaction derived from working on the case, would constitute adequate measures of the quality of the service given.

Respondents. It was anticipated that most of the respondents would be the mothers involved. This proved to be the case: 80% of the interviews were conducted with the mother only. Twelve percent were joint interviews with the mother and the father and the remaining 8% with the father alone. Where data were obtained from both sources, the mother's information was given precedence in coding. Feminine pronouns are used in the text but the reader should understand that the sample was not exclusively female. Feminine pronouns are also used in referring to the social workers although the percentage of males in this sample was high (27%).

Respondent Reliability. A study that relies heavily on data from respondents asked to give accounts of unacceptable social behavior inevitably raises questions about the validity of the data obtained. Such respondents would be expected to understate their problems and overstate their improvement, to some extent. These biases are reduced by sensitive interviewing methods but even the most skilled inter- viewers will have respondents who are evasive and whose stories contain contradictions and inconsistencies. To assess the magnitude of this problem, interviewers were asked to rate each respondent's reliability and, after reading the case record, to note discrepancies between the information given by the respondent, and by the worker in the agency's record.

The interviewers described 87% of the respondents as accepting the interview situation; only 13 (9%) were described as "somewhat hostile," and 9 (5%) as "very hostile" or "guarded." Similarly, only 11 (6%) were described as "very unreliable" but 43% were rated as "somewhat unreliable." The most common reason given for this rating was a sense that the respondent was "holding back" and not telling the full story. Half the respondents were considered wholly reliable.

The discrepancies between the respondent's story and the case record were noted and analyzed to determine whether they occurred at random or whether there was a pattern suggesting that certain kinds of data should be considered biased. The analysis indicated that in only 17% of the cases were there no factual discrepancies at all, while the

Table 1-1

Frequency of Discrepancies Between
Interview and Case Reading
n=171

Type of Discrepancy	%
Omissions related to agency	35
Omissions related to child	20
Omissions related to family	17
Omissions from case record	17
Understatement about agency-related problems	19
Understatement about parent-related problems	17
Understatement about child-related problems	15
Contradiction concerning agency	18
Contradiction concerning family	12
Contradiction concerning child	9
Exaggeration concerning agency	17
Exaggeration concerning family	9
Exaggeration concerning child	6
Confusion and uncertainty	18
Differences in interpretation of events	13
Discrepancies related to abuse/neglect	15

median number was two. Table 1.1 gives the type of discrepancy and the frequency of occurrences.

As the table indicates, the form of discrepancy that occurs with startlingly higher frequency than any other is the omission by the respondent related to agency activity. The most common of these (26 cases) was omission by the respondent of references to help offered or given by the protective services workers. In addition, references to activity prior to 1973, omissions of information about help offered or given by other agencies, and omissions about involvement of workers other than those described in the interview were not uncommon. Understatements, exaggerations and contradictions were also more likely to occur in relation to agency data as compared to data about the child or the family itself.

As the table indicates, discrepancies of any kind related to the abuse or neglect of the child occurred in only 26 cases (15%). Of these 14 (9%) involved cases in which the abuse or neglect charged was more severe than the respondent acknowledged in the interview.

Data Analysis. A code book was developed during the course of data collection and pretested. Coding was done by two coders under the supervision of the research associate. A 20% reliability check was made. The agreement rate, after training, averaged 85%.

After the data were keypunched and cleaned of errors, data reduction was achieved by developing indices reflecting various attitudes and outcomes. These are described, where appropriate, in Chapter III. Outcome variables were cross-tabulated against independent variables. Those variables showing a statistically significant relationship with an outcome variable were entered into a regression analysis to eliminate spurious relationships and to assess the relative impact of each variable on the degree of variance accounted for. Additional analysis was carried out, as reported in Chapter IV, on differences between abusive and neglectful parents.

Subsequent chapters in this report detail the principal findings, and discuss the problem of outcome variables, differences between abusive and neglecting parents, and variations in agency practice. The concluding chapter discusses the implications of the findings and their consistency or lack of consistency with other research findings and with the practice literature, and makes recommendations for future research and practice.

References

1. Young, Leontine. <u>Wednesday's Children</u>. New York: McGraw-Hill, 1964, p. 257.

2. Kadushin, Alfred. <u>Child Welfare Services</u>. New York: Macmillan, 2nd edition, 1974, p. 269.

3. Berkeley Planning Associates. Berkeley, Calif.: <u>Evaluation of Child Abuse and Neglect Demonstration Projects, 1974-1977, Volume III. Adult Client Impact; Final Report</u>, p. 11.

4. Baker, Jean M. <u>Parents Anonymous Self-Help for Child Abusing Parents Project</u>. Behavior Associates, Inc., Tucson (photocopy), 1976.

5. Kahn, Alfred J. "The Design of Research," in Norman Polansky (ed.) <u>Social Work Research</u>, 1st ed. Chicago: The University of Chicago Press, 1960, pp. 52-53.

6. Information from the agencies is based on their reports and on Child Welfare League Studies. Since these were done at different times for different purposes, the information given is not uniform.

7. Robinson, John, and Shaver, Philip. <u>Measures of Social Phsychological Attitudes</u>. Ann Arbor: Survey Research Center, Institute for Social Research, 1973, pp. 81-83.

Chapter II
THE FAMILIES

This chapter and the chapter that follows present the key characteristics of the study families, the nature of the charges of abuse and
neglect leveled against them, their response to the situation and the
services offered to them. Chapter II covers demographic variables and
describes the socioeconomic status of the families at the time of the
interview with respect to employment and housing. Their involvement
with the extended family and their social relations are also described.
The status of the children in each family in relation to health,
schooling, and relationship problems is described, as are parental views
on parenthood and parents' own childhood experiences. Chapter III
centers on the abuse and neglect problem that resulted in agency
involvement, the families' response to it and the characteristics of the
workers and the services they offered.

Family Composition. The single-parent/female-headed family
constituted 61% of the sample. Thirty-two percent of the families had
two parents at the time of the interview but the male parent was not
necessarily the father of the child. Seven percent of the families
consisted of single fathers and their children. Only 11 families in the
entire sample included an adult other than a parent and thus could be
considered extended.

In only 18% of the families was the biological father of the children the legal spouse of the mother and currently living with her. For the largest proportion (39%), he was divorced from the mother; in only a few instances (16% of those who were divorced) had he been replaced by a stepfather. Another 16% of the total sample were headed by mothers who had separated from the father after a legal marriage, while 10% were separated after a period of cohabitation. Again, in only 11% of the families where there had been a separation, was there a replacement by a stepparent, with or without a legal marriage. In 5% of the cases, the biological father was deceased. In the remaining 12% there was no information about him, and he had not been replaced by another male parent.

Figures from the case records on marital status recorded at the time of intake differ somewhat from the study data, but still convey the dominance of the female-headed family. Only 28% of the families in the study were headed by a married couple, according to the records. Thirty percent of the female heads of families were divorced and 23% separated. Twelve percent had never married and 6% were widowed.

The number of children reared in these families ranged from one to 12, with a median of three. Forty-four percent of the mothers had reared four or more children. In the largest group of families, all children were of school age or over. These families included 577 children, of whom 54% were boys and 46% girls. The total sample's age distribution is shown in Table 2-1.

In 61% of the families, all the children were in the home at the time of the interview. In 31%, some of the children were placed in foster homes, some were with relatives and others were at home. In the remaining 8%, all children were outside the home. In slightly more than half the families a major change in family composition had taken place in the 2 years covered by the interview. The most common (26%) involved the departure of the mother's spouse or paramour.

Table 2-1

Ages of Children in the Study

n=577

	%
Under 4	21
5-7	22
8-10	22
11-16	20
17 or over	15
	100

Mother's Age. Mothers ranged in age from 20 to 53, with a median age of 30. Eleven percent had started childbearing at 16 or earlier, the oldest at 33. The median age at the birth of the first child was 19.

As would be expected in a sample such as this, information about the father was frequently missing. The median age for the 125 fathers on whom data on age were available was 35, with a range from 20 to 75.

Race. Sixty-seven percent of the mothers in the study families were white, and 23% were black. The remainder were of Hispanic or Indian origin.

Socioeconomic Status. Slightly over half the population (53%) were wholly dependent on public funds and a little over a quarter (27%) on a combination of public funds and earnings. In only 14% of the families was the father's earnings the principal source of income. Mother's earnings accounted for 4%. For the remainder, the source of income was unclear. Of those families who were not on welfare, case readers made a judgment, on the basis of information in the record, that two-thirds had adequate means and that one-third were living on an inadequate or poverty level even though they were not receiving public funds.

Of the 61 fathers about whom employment information was given, and who were in the household, 14% were employed. Thirty-six percent were unemployed. Of the 69 who were not in the household, the large majority (71%) made only occasional contributions to their children's care. Of those who made regular contributions, most did so under a court order. Of the 95 employed fathers, the majority (78%) were in blue collar or unskilled occupations. As would be expected with this occupational level, of the 116 fathers on whom data were available 20% had an eighth-grade education or less. The largest proportion (35%) had some high school but did not graduate. Thirty-one percent had graduated from high school and an additional 14% had some education afterward.

Only 19% of the mothers were working at the time of the interview, nearly all in unskilled occupations, such as food service or factory work. They were about equally divided between those who worked full time and those who worked part time. Of those who were not working, the largest proportion (61%) indicated that it was possible they would look for work in the near future. Twenty percent had definite plans for vocational training or for employment, leaving only 18% with no apparent interest in the job market. When this latter group of mothers was asked why they were not employed, the largest proportion (33%) indicated that they were thinking about it or were looking but hadn't been able to find anything. Twenty-eight percent indicated that they had little skill or earning power or that there was no appropriate work in their communities and so had apparently resigned themselves to unemployment. Fourteen percent gave poor physical or mental health as their reason for unemployment. Nine percent said that it was not practical for them to work; expenses involved would outweigh their earning power. Only 4% said they had no suitable person to care for their children. It is particularly noteworthy that only 12% felt they were needed at home.

In addition to the 19% working currently, 68% of the mothers had been employed in the past. As expected, the majority had worked in unskilled occupations: food service, factory work, and domestic service. The rest had experience in a variety of semiskilled occupations of which the most common was the paraprofessional, such as nurse's or teacher's aide. The largest proportion of those who had been employed (48%) had an erratic work history, usually working for short periods in a variety of occupations. The experience of 29% was limited to a single job held before marriage or childbearing. Thirteen percent had never been employed.

Only 11% had a relatively stable work history or a clear identification with an occupational role. Of those who wanted to work, about half had aspirations for paraprofessional or professional training. The rest expected to continue in the types of unskilled work with which they were familiar.

The mothers' educational level paralleled that of the fathers, except that mothers were less likely to have completed high school. Twenty percent had an eighth-grade education or less. Forty-three percent had attended high school but had not graduated. Twenty-one percent had graduated from high school; 16% had some professional training or college beyond high school.

The mean income for these families, regardless of source, was $104 a week or an annual income of $5400, clearly at the poverty level. As Table 2-2 shows, only 20% of the families had an income of over $7400 a year.

Sixty percent of the families reported some increase in income during the 2- to 3- year period covered by the interview, mostly because of increase in welfare assistance (26%) or some increases in wages (18%). A third were moderately optimistic that they could increase their earning powers in the near future. Twenty percent were strongly optimistic, but a relatively large minority (42%) saw little or no chance of improvement in their economic position. Whatever optimism there

Table 2-2

Income of Study Families

n=171

	%
Under $2540	20
2541-4000	19
4001-5700	21
5701-7400	20
7401-20,800	20
	100

was stemmed from the expectation that the mother would be able to go to work or find a better job.

Housing. Half the respondents had lived at their current address for a year or less. A little over a third (37%) had lived there for 2 to 4 years. Only 12% had lived in the same place for over 4 years. The most common reason given for moving was to obtain larger quarters. In 8% of the cases, the move had to do with family conflict. For the rest, the the reasons were, in addition to larger quarters, other conditions also related to housing itself: reduced rent, more desirable or safer neighborhoods, or better quality. The large majority (75%) were satisfied that their current housing was better.

Consistent with this view of improvement were the high ratings given by the respondents on the general adequacy of their housing and specifically in relation to size, heat, state of repair, and absence of pests. Seventy-one percent rated their housing as adequate. Most were also satisfied with the state of transportation in their area and rated the neighborhood as fair or good. If this seems an unusually high degree of satisfaction for a poverty-level population, it should be noted that a big proportion (60%) presented housing problems at the time of intake (see Chapter III) and that many were helped or at least encouraged to move by their workers.

Case readers were asked to judge the adequacy of housing from the material in the record. In this instance, the degree of adequacy perceived is not quite as marked as that based on the interviews. Sixty-four percent of the families were seen as living in generally adequate housing. Details of the housing problems were not usually given, except for references to inadequate size. The difference in the general assessment can be attributed either to changes that took place later or a higher standard of adequacy held by the workers.

Housekeeping. Case readers decided on the basis of the records that about 28% of the respondents could be considered below average in their housekeeping ability. Forty-one percent were described as average and 22% as above average. For the remaining 8%, no information was available. Interviewer ratings tended to be somewhat more positive. Twenty-four percent rated their respondents' living quarters as very dirty or untidy, 36% as "average" and 35% as "clean" or "very attractive." The difference may be attributable either to actual improvement on the part of the respondent or to the fact that the one-time, by-appointment nature of the research interview made it easier for the respondent to make a good impression; the protective services workers who may visit more frequently and do so unannounced are more likely to see a lower level of housekeeping.

Experiences With Agencies. According to the respondents, their experiences with agency services before their involvement with protective services was usually limited to public assistance. Only 25% of the respondents had never received public assistance. The largest proportion (53%) had been on welfare before their involvement with protective services and continued afterward. Fourteen percent began to receive public assistance after the complaint was initiated, while 9% had received public assistance at some point in their earlier history but not at the time of the complaint. Other than this, relatively few acknowledged involvement with any type of social agency, independently of protective services. Only 21% reported contacts with agencies serving children, such as child guidance clinics, youth services, or educational programs such as Head Start, etc. Only 13 respondents (8%) had had any contact with child welfare agencies. In relation to agencies servicing adults, slightly more than a quarter (28%) acknowledged receiving services from any agency, the most common of which was a mental hygiene clinic.

Case record information was not as detailed as that given in the interview but confirmed the low level of involvement. Only 13% of the families were known to have had extensive involvement with other agencies. Sixty-one percent were said to be known to other agencies but apparently not for intensive services, while 26% had no contact of any kind. Of the agency contacts described in the records, mental hygiene services were also the most common, followed by medical services.

Social Relations. A series of questions was asked to determine the extent to which the respondents were helped by the extended family, friends or organizational affiliations. In the case of the extended family, only 8% of the respondents reported contact both with their parents and siblings. The next largest group (23%) reported contact with their parents only. An additional 19% reported contact only with sisters. The remaining 21% reported seeing other relatives or combinations other than parents and sister. Sixty percent indicated that their contacts were frequent (once a week or oftener) but most of the rest reported only minimal or occasional contact. Of those whose contact was minimal, half gave strained relations as the reason; less than a third claimed practical problems, such as geographic separation. The sample was about equally divided between those who described family relations as always good or improved over the past and those who described their relationships as mixed (good relations with some family members, strained relations with others) or always hostile.

The helpfulness of the extended family varied considerably. Thirty-two percent of the respondents reported that relatives gave some help with child care. Of these, about half gave financial or material help as well. Twelve percent gave financial help only. Twenty-eight percent reported that the extended family gave only moral support and the same proportion reported that the extended family gave no help at all.

Case records also indicated that the study families were relatively isolated from the extended family. For 39%, there was evidence of a strong attachment to at least one member of the family, most often the maternal grandmother. In 32%, there were indications of occasional contact. Twenty-one percent were known to have little or no contact. For the remaining 8% there was no information in the record.

Neighbors were not usually seen as a resource for help. When questioned, 26% of the respondents reported no contact or acquaintance with neighbors at all. A slightly larger proportion (30%) saw the neighbors as acquaintances only. Eleven percent regarded the neighbors as friends but did not involve them in any of their problems. Twenty percent reported that the neighbors were helpful with their children and an additional 13% reported that the neighbors gave other forms of help. The most common reason given for lack of contact was the respondent s view of herself as a reserved, shy person who found it difficult or embarrassing to make contact with others and preferred privacy.

Organizations were even less likely to be seen as a resource. When questioned, more than half the sample (56%) said they had no organizational affiliations at all. Of those who had, church membership was mentioned much more frequently than any other form of affiliation (30% of the total sample or 73% of those who had organizational affilia- tions). No other organization--community groups, parent groups, recreational organizations, etc.--was mentioned by more than a handful of respondents. The most common reason given for inactivity was lack of time, but the respondent's characterization of herself as "not a joiner" was almost as common. Almost no organization, including the church, was rated as helpful in relation to any of the problems the respondents had.

When asked how frequently they managed to get out and enjoy some social life, 27% of the respondents said they had no social life at all. Another 13% described participation in social events as only occasional (every few months). Twenty-four percent said they managed to get out "fairly often" (once a month or so). Only 36% described a regular social life, permitting them to get out at least once a week.

The type of social life described was quite varied, with nearly equal proportions reporting going to the movies (18%), visiting friends (18%), going to bars (17%) or visiting relatives (15%). The remainder went to parks, attended organized games, went to dances, parties, or athletic events.

Reasons for a limited social life differed somewhat from the reasons for lack of contact with neighbors. Here the emphasis tended to be on practical obstacles, such as the expense and lack of sitters, but a substantial minority (32%) said they wanted no social life, were afraid of new people, had no friends, or no energy, or felt out of place among the people they knew.

Of those who had some social life, the largest group (28%) left their children in the care of a relative or spouse. The next largest group (20%) confined their social activities to their own homes and so eliminated the problem of child care. Fifteen percent took their children along wherever they went and a similar proportion (14%) had neighbors or friends sit for them. Only 11% used paid babysitters. Nine percent left younger children in the care of older ones, while the remaining 37% considered their children old enough to remain by themselves.

Reviewing all the information given by respondents about their contacts outside the immediate family, research staff judged that a third of the respondents led an apparently normal social life. Fifty-four percent were seen as somewhat isolated and 13% exceptionally so. If one compares the various forms of social relations, it is evident that isolation is greatest in relation to neighbors and to formal organizations; less extensive but still substantial in relation to the extended family and to informal social life.[1]

Children. Respondents were asked to describe the health, school status, and relationships with peers and adults of each of the children they had reared. The incidence of problems, taking into account all the children in the family, was reported as shown in Table 2-3.

Table 2-3

Child-Related Problems in Study Families[2]

n=171

	%
Health	47
Relationships with significant adults*	40
School**	36
Relationships with siblings	34
Relationships with peers	22

*Teachers, relatives other than parents, etc.
**Both performance and behavior problems

Thus every category of problem, with the exception of peer relations, affected at least a third of these families. Specific types of problems were identified in the analysis but no clear pattern emerged. Problems were diversified and seemed to include most common childrearing problems. Parents were also asked how they coped with each problem named. Their reactions or methods of handling problems are reported in Table 2-4 in order of frequency.

The high incidence of discussion with others probably stems from the fact that this population has been receiving service. It is worth noting that although these parents have been publicly accused of maltreating their children, a third acknowledged the use of physical punishment, a method of coping that in its extreme form obviously leads to child abuse.

Table 2-4

Methods of Coping With Child-Related Problems[3]

n=171

	%
Involving others (consulting social workers, teachers, friends)	77
Mild verbal methods ("talking to the child")	36
Evasion ("let them fight it out")	32
Physical punishment	32
Helplessness (no idea what to do)	25
Isolation (making child stay in room)	23
Strong verbal methods (scolding)	22
Deprivation (taking away privileges)	17

When they had completed their descriptions of individual children, respondents were asked: "It's always tough to be a parent; how do you feel about it?" They were asked to specify any differences in feelings about parenting since the complaint. The largest group saw no change (30%), but an almost equal proportion saw their parenting capacities as much better (29%) or somewhat better. Very few saw themselves as having deteriorated in this respect. Of those who described improvement, the most frequent responses were that they had gained greater maturity (18%), were happier with themselves (15%), were better able to accept responsibility (15%), and felt better about being a parent (12%). From the general discussion of their feelings about the parenting role, the largest group (43%) described mixed feelings. They had some satisfactions but were conscious of the responsibilities and demands of parenthood. Nearly half were described as generally accepting and, of these, many spoke in strongly positive terms, saying, for example, that being a parent was the greatest source of satisfaction in their lives.

Only 10% could be described as clearly rejecting the parental role, with such statements as "I should never have been a parent to begin with."

When asked to name the most important thing about being a mother, the largest proportion said "care of the home" (34%), with "giving love" (20%) named second most frequently. Respondents were asked the same question in relation to the fathers' role, but their answers indicated that they made relatively few distinctions between the two roles.

Childrearing Measures. Additional measures of attitudes toward childrearing were introduced in an effort to determine whether they could constitute a measure of authoritarianism and might distinguish between abusive and neglectful families in ways suggested by the literature. Analysis indicated that these items, which were original with the study and had not been previously tested, did not correlate with one another, did not differentiate either between abusive and neglectful parents or those who improved and those who did not (with a single exception to be reported in Chapter IV). The overall response is reported here since it gives some indication of the attitudes taken by the study parents on a number of significant aspects of childrearing.

Items on which there was relative consensus are shown in Table 2-5.

Items on which there was much less consensus are shown in Table 2-6.

The items on which there was relative consensus suggest that the parents do not have permissive attitudes, are inclined toward strict supervision and to profess high standards of child care. The items on which consensus is lacking may be subject to different interpretations or lack the same significance for the respondent that they had for the researcher. It is also possible that some of these responses represent genuine confusion or uncertainty about how strict parents should be. It is noteworthy that the parents are not advocates of physical punishment

Table 2-5

Childrearing Attitudes: Consensus

	Agree Strongly %	Agree Somewhat %	Disagree Somewhat %	Disagree Strongly %
Parents should make sure a child gets to school every day	82	13	3	2
Taking away privileges is a better form of punishment than hitting	52	35	7	5
Children should obey immediately when told to do something	37	34	22	7
It's not important how a child is dressed	14	11	57	18
Children should be punished whenever they disturb their parents	10	14	24	52
It doesn't matter whether a child gets his meals at regular times as long as he gets enough food	17	24	16	43

even though a third acknowledge using it.[4] Whether such confusion or uncertainty was part of the respondent's problem initially or whether it represents part of the response to service is hard to say.

Early Attitudes. Case readers were asked to note whether there was any early indication that mothers had rejected in infancy the children they were charged with abusing or neglecting. Case readers found information on this point in only 59 records. In 22% of these cases, they saw evidence of overt or implicit rejection. In 25%, the mother was described as ambivalent--sometimes rejecting and sometimes more accepting. For 29%, the record indicated that the mother's attitude varied with the child--some were rejected, others better

Table 2-6

Childrearing Attitudes: Nonconsensus

	Agree Strongly %	Agree Somewhat %	Disagree Somewhat %	Disagree Strongly %
Older children should be responsible for younger children	17	31	23	29
Babies will be spoiled if they are picked up whenever they cry	39	26	14	21
Spanking and hitting are very important in training children	8	34	30	28
Children should learn not to make a lot of noise when they are in the house	16	40	25	19

accepted. The remaining 24% were described as accepting their children during infancy.

Mother's Childhood. Asked to describe their childhood experiences, the respondents' responses reflected a fairly even spread, ranging from those who suffered much deprivation and had severe problems in growing up, to those who considered their childhoods to have been relatively happy. The proportion of those giving childhood histories of serious problems was about equal (33%) to those giving essentially positive descriptions of their earlier life experiences (30%). Some (24%) gave descriptions that included major problems but indicated these were offset by positive factors ("We were very poor but my parents did their best for us."). A small proportion (13%) made claims to a happy childhood but the interview contained evidence that suggested that this was an overstatement or an attempt to deny problems.[5]

The positive aspect of childhood most frequently specified was adequate physical care (40%), followed by concerned or loving parents

(27%). The majority (54%) saw the principal mother figure in their lives as a good parent ("I was brought up right"), but a substantial minority (37%) clearly rejected their mother figures as role models ("I don't want to raise my children the way my mother raised me"). The remaining 9% perceived the mother figure's failings but defended them and did not seem to lack identification with them ("I got beatings but it was good for me").

A content analysis of the childhood problems named by the respondents showed the frequency with which they occurred in this sample. (Table 2-7)

Table 2-7
Childhood Problems of Abusive/Neglectful Parents
n=171

	%
Excessive demands/restrictions	39
Physical or psychological absence of parent	29
Lack of love/parental indifference	27
Pressure to escape from home	19
Deprivation/neglect	19
Frequent, severe physical punishment	16
Death of parent	15
Multiple parenting	12
Premature/excessive responsibility	12
Sibling rivalry	12
Alcoholic parents	11
Chronic conflict in home	11

It is particularly noteworthy that only 16% reported frequent and severe physical punishment in childhood and thus might have been considered abused. The majority (51%) reported that physical punishment was used only occasionally or with a frequency or severity that did not appear excessive in the respondent's eyes. The remainder reported little or no physical punishment. This response may very well have been understated, but it seems clear that most respondents did not perceive themselves as abused children.[6]

Only about a third of the case records gave any information on whether the mother had been abused or neglected. In the 63 cases where there was information, 32% were described as neglected, 22% as abused, and 29% as both. For the remaining 19% the nature of the problems was unclear. There was no material of any kind on the mother's history in 81 (48%) of the records. Of the 90 cases where problems were described, 70 were seen as major and 15 as secondary. In only five records was there a direct statement that the mother's childhood was relatively free of problems.

Like the information given by the respondents in the interview, excessive restrictions emerged as the most commonly named childhood problem in those records where history material was found, but the incidence of other problems was quite different, as Table 2-8 shows.

Table 2-8

Mother's Childhood Problems as Described

in the Case Record

n=90

	%
Excessive restrictions	39
Rejection/lack of love	27
Premature adulthood*	22
Childhood medical/psychiatric problems	22
Multiple mothering	20
In foster care	19
Absence of parent	17

*Teen pregnancy or marriage

Incidence of Pathology. On the basis of information in the case records, the mothers in slightly under half the families appeared to be in reasonably good mental health. For the half where there was evidence of disturbance, instances were of an unspecified, undiagnosed nature. Drug or alcohol addiction was mentioned in 17 and depression in 14. Seven mothers were described as retarded and six as psychotic. Medical problems were indicated for 23 mothers, about evenly divided between serious, chronic problems, and those of a more transient nature. For the 50 families in which information was available on the father's health, alcoholism was mentioned in half.

Stress Factors. Another way of looking at family problems was to list the stress factors used in the National Clearinghouse Form and note the frequency with which they occurred in the case records. This was done primarily to permit comparability with the Clearinghouse figures. Of the 17 factors, a median of 4.5 stresses was checked for each family. For only a quarter of the families were three or fewer stresses listed. In descending order of frequency, the most common are shown in Table 2-9.

Other problems in the list--such as debts, work stability, use of drugs other than alcohol, mental retardation, mental illness, poor work habits, new babies, new pregnancies, physical abuse of spouse, recent relocation, police records, newcomers to the household, use of physical discipline as a normal method of childrearing--occurred with considerably less frequency than any of those listed in the table.

Personality. Since extensive personality testing was not possible in the context of this study, the most feasible method of obtaining a relatively objective assessment was the introduction of the self-administered questionnaire of the Rosenberg Self-Esteem Scale.[7] Scores for this scale have not been standardized, but the general response indicated that most study subjects felt a relatively high sense of self-esteem. (Table 2-10)

Apparently many respondents did not feel entirely satisfied with themselves, wished they could have more respect for themselves, and

Table 2-9

Frequency of Family Stress as Seen in Case Records

n=171

	%
Marital	57
Continuous childbearing	46
Alcoholism	36
Absence of essential family member	36
Unemployment	35
Insufficient income	35
Repetition of life style*	33
Physical illness	22
Misuse of income	21

*Long-term pattern of deviant behavior

Table 2-10

Responses on Rosenberg Self-Esteem Scale

n=171

	Agree Strongly %
I feel that I have a number of good qualities	72
I feel that I am a person of worth	69
I am able to do things as well as most other people	64
On the whole, I am satisfied with myself	47

	Disagree Strongly %
I feel that I do not have much to be proud of	64
All in all, I'm inclined to feel that I am a failure	62
At times I think I am no good at all	54
I wish I could have more respect for myself	35
I certainly feel useless at times	26

often felt useless. But, other than this, they did not seem to have as low an opinion of themselves as might have been expected in view of their circumstances. When these items were combined into an index, the scores were divided evenly among those which were relatively high. average, and relatively low. As will be seen in Chapter IV, these differences were not related to the extent to which respondents improved, and they did not differentiate between abusive and neglectful parents.

Summary. The study sample included predominantly female-headed, single-parent families with a median of three children. Mothers were typically about 30 years old and had started childbearing at 19. The families were heavily dependent on public funds or on earnings that placed them at the poverty level. The mothers had worked at unskilled occupations, had some interest in returning to the job market but seemed to have few resources for doing so. They seemed fairly pessimistic about the possibility for changes in the future. Despite the low socioeconomic level at which they lived, they were generally satisfied with their housing. Their recent histories were characterized by many forms of stress, particularly marital. Chronic pathology was present for a substantial minority, but no one form was predominant. Their principal contacts were with a few members of the extended family and with friends. Contacts with neighbors and organizational affiliations were limited.

Health, school and relationship problems were commonly reported for many of the children in these families. In coping with their child-rearing problems, these mothers consulted others, "talked" to their children, and resorted to physical punishment. Their attitude toward parenting was typically mixed, involving some satisfaction but aware-ness of the responsibilities and difficulties of childrearing. Their expressions of values emphasized physical care somewhat more strongly than emotional support. Descriptions of their childhood experiences varied from the relatively comfortable to the severely traumatic, but histories of child abuse were not frequently reported.

Notes and References

1. This pattern of isolation, whether from the extended family or the community, continues to be noted in many ot the newer studies, as well as the older ones, including those having comparison groups. It is reported in the 1977 Analysis of Child Abuse and Neglect Research, issued by the National Center on Child Abuse and Neglect, pp. 16/17, as well as in Milton Kotelchuck, "Child Abuse: Prediction and Misclassification," (photocopy), 1977, pp. 15-17, and in Norman Polansky et al., "The Isolation of the Neglected Family" (photocopy), 1978, pp. 19-20.

2. Percentages for Tables 2-3 and 2-4 total higher than 100 since multiple problems and multiple methods of coping were named by many respondents.

3. Nearly all health problems were dealt with by obtaining some form of medical care. Ignoring a medical problem or using home remedies occurred only in isolated cases. Coping methods in Table 2-4 therefore refer to school and relationship problems.

4. A similar pattern appeared in the League's recently completed study of childrearing among white mothers. Spankings were used by 92% of the study mothers but there was no consensus about the effectiveness of this method as a means of disciplining children. (Lucille Grow, in press.)

5. A similar question addressed to participants in the Parents Anonymous program showed a response pattern that leaned more heavily in the direction of describing childhood as unhappy (46%): Jean M. Baker, Parents Anonymous Self-Help for Child Abusing Parents Project, Behavior Associates, Inc., 1977, (photocopy), p. 69.

6. The Baker report, op. cit., p. 72, cites 11% of the parents in its sample as reporting physical abuse as the most serious problem during their childhood. Jayaratne, in "Child Abusers as Parents and Children, a Review," Social Work, January, 1977, pp. 5-9, cites Gil's figure (in Violence Against Children, Harvard University Press, 1970, p. 138) as 14% and describes the general lack of convincing evidence for the generational hypothesis commonly advanced in discussions on child abuse.

7. John Robinson and Philip Shaver, Measures of Social Psychological Attitudes, Survey Research Center, Institute for Social Research, University of Michigan, 1970, p. 281.

Chapter III
PROTECTIVE SERVICES

Chapter II has given us a picture of a study sample of poor families beset by many of the problems common to low income populations. This chapter will describe the complaints of abuse or neglect made against these families, their response to the complaints, the types of help given them and the families' response.

The Complaint. According to agency records, 57% of the respondents came to the attention of the agency as the result of complaints of neglect, 25% for abuse, and 13% for both.[1] Five percent were referred for service because a potential was apparently perceived for abuse or neglect. In the parents' version of the events leading to the referral, 30% did not directly acknowledge any complaint. Some said that they or a member of the family had asked for service or that they had been referred by other agencies. Of the 120 who did admit to a complaint, 65% described it as neglect, 31% as abuse and 4% as both.

The sample was evenly divided between those cases in which the complaint was focused on all children in the family and those where the complaint involved one or more but not all children. According to agency records, the mother alone was the alleged perpetrator in 51% of the families, both parents in 25%, the father alone in 11%. In isolated cases, the perpetrator was the mother in combination with others, usually a paramour. In a few instances, the perpetrator was a stepparent, a sibling, or foster parents.

Again, according to agency record, the single most common source of referral was a social agency, involved in 28% of the cases. Relatives, schools, and neighbors accounted for equal proportions of the referrals: 13% each. Nurses accounted for 8%, doctors for 6%, the police for 5%. Parents referred themselves in 5% and spouses in 2% of the cases. For the remaining 7%, the records gave no indication of the referral source. Thus, approximately 60% of the referrals came from the representatives of social institutions, while 34% were from individuals.

In the parents' own version of these events, 12% of those who acknowledged a complaint said they did not know its source. Of those who both acknowledged the complaint and named a source, 44% named institutional settings, of which the most common was a hospital clinic. Fifty-six percent named individuals. It seems evident that parents are more aware or suspicious of individuals as sources of complaints than they are of institutional sources.[2]

According to agency records, the complaint in question was the first one made for 50% of the sample. In 25%, there was a history of a previous complaint, usually more than 2 years earlier. For 19%, another complaint followed the one that determined inclusion in the study. For 6%, there were both previous and subsequent complaints.

Among the specific abuse complaints, beatings were the most common (42% of the 64), followed by cuts and bruises (23%). There were two or three complaints each of sexual abuse, bone fractures, homicidal attacks (attempts to choke the child), and burns. Of the 121 neglect complaints, the most common was a general inadequacy characterized by multiple complaints. This accounted for 43% of the cases. Lack of supervision was specified in 11%, emotional neglect in another 11%, educational neglect and failure to thrive in 6% each, and medical neglect and abandonment in 5% each. Seven percent were cases in which the referral source saw a strong potential for neglect in a drug-addicted or alcoholic parent. In the remaining 6%, the nature of the complaint was unclear.

Of those respondents who acknowledged that there had been a complaint, the largest group (36%) admitted directly that the complaint was valid. The remainder were about equally divided between those who explicitly denied it, those who made a tacit admission and those who neither denied nor admitted it. Not surprisingly, the largest group of respondents (30%) expressed anger and resentment at the complaint, but the next highest proportion (20%) reported relief and acceptance. The rest expressed feelings of upset (13%), bewilderment and shock (9%), fear (9%), a sense of harassment (3%), or depression (2%). Six percent expressed no feelings at all. In the remaining cases, the respondent initiated the complaint, usuallly against a spouse.

In assessing all the available data, research staff considered that the validity of the complaint was established in 75%; there was some room for doubt in the remaining 25%. As will be seen in Chapter V, the sample was divided for analytic purposes into three groups: marginal (25%), neglectful (48%), abusive (27%). Those who were both abusive and neglectful were included in the last category.

Role of the Court. Only 29% of the respondents were involved in court hearings on formal charges of either abuse or neglect. Fifty percent, however, had been involved in some other kind of court action, and a third of the sample had been involved in more than one. After abuse or neglect hearings, the most common forms of court action were custody disputes, followed by criminal cases involving the parents, and delinquency proceedings involving some of the children. Of those parents who had not been involved in court action, slightly more than half were confident that they would not be, or denied that there was any likelihood of such an action. The rest did acknowledge some apprehension, including a few who indicated that threats of court action had been made by the agency or by members of the family.

Not surprisingly, the most common feelings reported by the respondents who were involved in court action were fear and a sense of being threatened. Over half the respondents affected indicated that they were unaware of any involvement on the part of protective services workers. Only 20% reported that workers testified, and an additional 20% said that the workers initiated the proceedings. In only five cases was testimony taken from professionals other than protective services workers.

The most common problem named by the respondents describing court proceedings was their inability to understand what was happening. Indifference or bias on the part of the judge was also occasionally mentioned.

Perception of the Worker's Objective. Respondents were asked how they perceived the worker's objective at the time of the complaint. The largest proportion (35%) saw the worker's objective in neutral terms, i.e., the worker was there to evaluate the problem. Almost as many saw the worker's objective in positive terms--she was there to offer help. A fairly large minority however (23%), saw the worker's purpose as hostile--she was there to "take the children away" or to get the parent to admit guilt.

The most commonly described initial general activity was a discussion of the family's problems and the offer of suggestions for help. The most commonly described specific action was placement in foster care (24%), followed by referrals of parents for psychiatric care (8%). Only 13% of the families said that the worker threatened court action. An additional 8% of the workers were said to have made passing references to court action of a nonthreatening nature, but the large majority made no reference to it at all.

When parents were asked what they thought the worker wanted them to do, the responses varied considerably. The most frequent was "to get myself straightened out" or to get treatment (18%), followed by agreeing to placement (12%), getting help for the child (11%), and taking care of the house and children (10%). Other expectations perceived were a greater degree of involvement with the children, "straightening out" marital problems, understanding the child better, or having a better self-image. A few thought the worker expected them to remove the abusive spouse or paramour. Others thought they were expected to adjust to the removal of a child, or confess guilt.

Most respondents (69%) said that their initial reaction to the worker's actions was one of gratitude and a willing acceptance of whatever suggestions had been made. A minority (15%) said they were defiant and claimed they saw no need for the course of action the worker suggested. A few (16%) said they followed suggestions because they felt they had to do so or they were frightened or confused. Most (60%) claimed they were honest and open about their feelings with the worker, but a substantial minority (26%) acknowledged feelings of distance, discomfort and anger.

In relation to the children, the most common action taken by the worker was an arrangement for foster care, followed by arrangements for medical care or psychotherapy for the parents of the children, arrangements for relatives to care for children, or day care. In relation to the family, general support and help in assuming responsibility for the children were most frequently described (37%). This was followed closely by referrals for more specific help, such as financial assistance, homemakers, and psychotherapy (34%).

The Workers. Forty percent of the families indicated that they had only one worker, but an almost equal proportion (37%) named two. Twenty-three percent named three or more workers. According to case records, 32% had one worker, 36% had two, and the remaining 34% had three or more. As was noted in Chapter I, underestimating the number of workers was an error made by many families.

To simplify the analytic process, information was coded for the worker designated as "major," i.e., the worker who invested the most time, made the key decisions, and seemed most involved with the family. Most often, the major worker was the first assigned to the case (51%), but in some instances she was the second (26%), the third (16%), and in a few cases (5%), even the fourth or the fifth. In the remaining 2%, worker status was unclear.

The major worker served the family for a median period of 16 months. Slightly over a third of the respondents described their feelings about the major worker as initially and consistently positive; an equal proportion described feelings that changed from neutral or negative to positive. A minority (24%) held consistently negative or neutral attitudes.

In general, the worker population appeared fairly typical for social work staff in public agencies. Typically, families were served by female workers under 35, white, childless, college graduates, without advanced training in social work.

Most workers had 3 years or less experience in protective services; over a third had no other social work experience. Of those with experience outside of protective services, nearly half had worked in other child welfare fields, such as foster care and adoption.

Most carried a specialized caseload, dealing only with complaints of abuse or neglect. The rest carried protective responsibilities as part of a general child welfare caseload. The median number of all families reported in these caseloads was 23.

Nature of Services. The agencies involved in the study were able to offer the families in the sample a range of services that included all or most of those that are part of the usual network of services found in most urban areas: foster care, day care, financial assistance, medical care, housing, mental hygiene clinics, employment training programs, etc. For the purposes of analysis, these services could be divided into two broad categories: those that provided some relief from the task of parenting by removing the children from the home on a 24-hour or daily basis, and those that supported the parents in their task while leaving the children in the home under agency supervision. Many parents were offered and received a combination of both types of service, but for greater clarity these will be described separately.

Relief of Parenting. Some form of relief from the parenting role was offered and accepted by 62% of the study sample, as Table 3-1 indicates:

Table 3-1

Services Providing Relief of Parenting

n=171

	%
Agency foster home	21
Relatives' care	9
Institution or group home	8
Day care	8
Combination of the above	15
Summer program	1
Counseling and other income services only	38
	100

Of the 74 cases involving placement of siblings, 63% required different placements. In only 35% was it possible to make the same placement plan for all siblings. The most common reason given for different placements was related to the special needs of one of the children, not the lack of available homes for sibling placements.

Of the families that were given this form of service, half reported relief and acceptance of the decision. About a quarter reported resentment and anger. A few reported guilt, worry or embarrassment. As part of the positive view of placement, more than half reported that the child's caretaker was supportive and helpful. About a third described the caretaker in hostile terms--incompetent, rejecting (of themselves or the children), bossy or competitive, rigid and demanding.

Despite acceptance of the need for this service, initial feelings upon separation were described in positive terms by only 36%. The rest described such negative feelings (in order) as depression, fear, anger, hurt and confusion. The largest proportion (42%) reported that their feelings about placement became more positive over time. More than a quarter, however, (26%) reported that their feelings about the placement remained consistently negative.

The majority of the children involved (70%) experienced only one uninterrupted placement and most were visited by their parents during placement. The median period of placement was 12 months. Twenty-nine percent of the children in these families spent 6 months or less in care. Thirty-six percent spent between 6 months and 2 years. The remaining 35% spent over 2 years and up to 38 months.

The majority of the parents (56%) reported no negative reactions on the part of their children to the placement. Twelve percent reported some adjustment problems that were later resolved, but a larger group (32%) thought their children had been harmed by the experience. In those instances where children were still in placement at the time of the interview, the parents had little expectation that they would return and expressed resignation about their status. For those who had been returned home, the parents were almost equally divided between those who thought the period of placement was "just right" in meeting their needs and those who thought the placement was unnecessarily long. Only one parent thought the placement was too short. Slightly over half the parents rated the placement experience as helpful. A substantial minority (29%) said it helped in some ways, but hurt in others, while 19% described it as unhelpful or even harmful. Of those who gave the experience a positive evaluation, the most common explanation was that placement had given the parent "a chance to get herself together." The most common reason for a negative assessment was the "bad influence" of the caretaker or the parent's inability to accept the separation.

Two other forms of relief of parenting responsibility were less frequently used--relatives' homes and day care. Nevertheless, both forms of service received more positive ratings from repondents than did foster care. In 13 of the 21 families where children were placed with relatives, the respondent rated the service as helpful. and in all but two of the 23 families where day care was used, the service was rated as very helpful. Surprisingly, for this sample, the most common reason given for the helpfulness of day care was that it provided a learning experience for the child.

It may also be noteworthy that, of these forms of relief of parenting responsibility, care by relatives had the highest rejection rate. Of the 69 families where care of the children by relatives was suggested by the worker, 28% refused in contrast to a 23% refusal rate for day care, and 20% for foster care. One might speculate that foster care was least likely to be refused because its use was reinforced by the authority of the protective services worker. Parents evidently were better able to refuse relative care or day care if they wished to do so but when they did accept it, were more likely to be satisfied than they were when they felt compelled to accept foster care. In view of the frequency of strained relations with the extended family, embarrassment or shame about asking for their help may also have been a contributing factor to the relatively high refusal rate. If relations with the extended family happened to be good, the parents' satisfaction with the relatives, care is self-explanatory.

Inhome Services. At least one service to assist the family while maintaining the children at home was offered to 72% of the families. The median number of services suggested was three. For 20% of the study families, at least one form of suggested service proved to be unavailable, while for 27% at least one service was refused. Thus, resistance to service was apparently a somewhat more common problem in working with this sample of families than was the availability of resources.

Information was secured for nine different forms of service in relation to their availability, respondents' willingness to use them, and actual use. Ratings were also given by each respondent on the extent to which they were perceived as helpful.

Table 3-2 gives the rank order in which each of these types of service was considered, proved unavailable, or was refused; then the proportion of actual usage is shown, followed by rank order of the extent to which the clients considered the service helpful.

Percentages in the first column are based on the total sample; for the next three columns the percentage is based on the number of cases where the service was considered appropriate, and for the column on the far right, the percentage is based on the cases where the service was actually used.

In general, one can say that homemakers, medical care, and mental hygiene clinics were the services most likely to be considered for these families; the services least likely to be considered were educational programs, recreational services, and parent groups. Problems of availability existed principally for educational and recreational resources. Medical services, homemakers, and mental hygiene services were nearly always available.

Refusal rates were highest for parent groups, mental hygiene servcies and homemakers; medical care, financial assistance, and the service of case aides were least likely to be refused. The highest actual rate of usage is apparently related to services involving physical or material needs--medical care, financial assistance, and housing. Medical services were also most likely to be rated as helpful, along with recreational services. Mental hygiene services, homemakers, and educational services were most likely to have "mixed reviews" from respondents. Reasons for refusals and for negative ratings of services were elicited but these seemed to be highly individual, and with the relatively small number of respondents involved in each service, no clear pattern emerged from the analysis.

Table 3-2

Use of Inhome Services

Cases in Which Service* Was Considered	%	Service** Unavailable	%	Service** Refused	%
Homemaker	45	Adult Education	32	Parent Groups	28
Medical Care	36	Recreation	32	Mental Hygiene	27
Mental Hygiene	35	Case Aides	29	Homemaker	23
Financial Assistance	30	Parent Groups	19	Employment	15
Housing	27	Housing	15	Housing	11
Case Aides	25	Financial Assistance	12	Recreation	5
				Medical Care	5
Employment	16	Employment	11	Adult Education	5
Adult Education	13	Medical Care	05	Financial Assistance	4
Recreation	11	Homemaker	4		
Parent Groups	11	Mental Hygiene	2	Case Aides	0

Service** Used	%	Service*** Evaluated as Very Helpful	%
Medical Care	90	Medical Care	91
Financial Assistance	83	Recreation	87
Housing	72	Case Aides	77
Mental Hygiene	72	Housing	77
Case Aides	71	Financial Assistance	76
Homemaker	70	Parent Groups	63
Employment	63	Mental Hygiene	57
Recreation	63	Homemaker	55
Adult Education	59	Adult Education	54
Parent Groups	52	Employment	41

*   Each percentage is based on the total number of families (171).

Figures add to more than 100% because more than one service was considered for each family.

** Each percentage is based on those cases where the service was considered.

*** Each percentage is based on those cases where the service was actually given.

When asked how they perceived the services offered, a small proportion saw them in negative terms, i.e., as a threat to their authority over their children. The largest group (43%) expressed mixed feelings--some services were seen as a threat, others not. Thirty-nine percent saw all the services offered in positive terms, as forms of help. The majority (77%) did not change these perceptions during the period of service; only 17% became more positive over time, while 6% became more negative. The most common reason for acceptance was need for relief of stress. Obtaining service for a child, such as medical or psychiatric care, was the next most frequent reason given for acceptance. Inability to manage the household or control the children was also reported with some frequency.

When respondents were asked what the service accomplished for their children, the most common response was that good care for their children was assured during a period of crisis. The next most frequently named accomplishment was obtaining treatment for the child. In terms of adult needs, obtaining treatment was even more frequently named as an "accomplishment" of protective services than it was for children (50%), with relief of pressure (25%) ranked second. Psychological changes such as improved family relations, help with behavior problems, and improving parenting capacity were infrequently mentioned. It is evident that the respondents most valued the enabling role played by the protective services worker in gaining access to material help. Help from the worker in changing parent-child relations was either not the primary desire, or the need was not perceived.

Overall Evaluation. Asked to summarize their feelings about their experience with protective services as a whole, respondents gave the ratings shown in Table 3-3.

Table 3-3

Respondent Rating of Protective Services

n=171

	%
Very positive	26
Positive	33
Neutral	8
Mixed (some aspects good, some not)	17
Negative	5
Strongly negative	9
No information	2
	100

The sample was about evenly divided between those who maintained the same attitudes (positive or negative) over the entire period covered and those who changed. Of the latter, the largest group (39%) took an increasingly positive view of their experience; relatively few changed in the opposite direction. The most common reason for a positive evaluation was the concern shown by the worker. The most common reason for a negative evaluation was the failure on the worker's part to give help that was meaningful to the client.

Agency Activity. The median period of agency activity was 2 years. Sixteen percent of the respondents had been known to the agencies before the complaints that had initiated the activity covered by the study. Most of these had been known to the agency for less than a year.

At the time of the interview, 53% of the cases had been closed with the agency; 45% were still active; the remaining 2% had been

transferred to other departments. Thirty-eight percent of the population had no one worker for longer than a year; at the other extreme,
only 20% had a single worker who served them for 2 years or more.

The first worker served a median period of 7 months. Thirty-three
percent who served less than 7 months did so for only a month and are
most likely to have been intake workers. If one disregards this latter
group, the median period of service for the first worker was 11 months.
Where there was a second worker, the median period of service was 10
months. The median for the longest period of time served by any
worker, regardless of when she was assigned, was 17 months.[4] In half
the cases, the worker designated in the interview as the major or most
influential worker was the first assigned. In 26% of the cases, it was
the second worker, and in 16%, it was the third. In the few remaining
cases, the fourth or fifth worker was designated as the major worker.

The case reader recorded the number of interviews, home visits,
office interviews, phone calls to families, contacts with social workers,
foster parents, homemakers, supervisors and other staff, calls to outside
agencies, staff conferences and court appearances. The findings
indicated that worker activity consisted heavily of home visits, phone
calls to families, and phone calls to other agencies. All other forms of
activity were relatively infrequent or under-recorded. All but six
families were visted at home at least once. The median number of
visits was 24; some families were visited as many as 95 times. The
average number of visits during the period the case was active was 1.3 a
month.

Somewhat less than half the families (43%) were never seen in the
agency's office. Of those who did have office interviews, very few had
more than one or two. No supervisory conferences were reported in
44% of the cases; for those where conferences were reported, the
median number was 10. Referral letters were written in 63% of the
cases. Five or more such letters were written in 30% of the cases.
Fifty-nine percent of the cases required at least one formal report; 19%

required five or more. Other forms of activity, such as conferences with foster parents, homemakers, psychiatric consultants, psychologists, seemed to have been the exception rather than the rule. As noted earlier, court appearances were not common for the workers on these cases. None were reported for 62% of the families and only one or two for the remainder.

Quality of Service. As experienced protective services workers, interviewers were asked to judge the quality of service given. In 23% of the cases, service was rated as very good, and in 32% as good; but in the largest proportion the service given was rated as routine (37%), with the remaining 7% evaluated as below average or poor. According to the interviewer, the worker's approach in the largest group of cases (46%) was described as supportive, but in almost as many (45%) it was described as combining both a supportive and an authoritarian approach. In only 6% were the workers seen primarily as authoritarian; the remainder could not be classified.

Supervisors were also asked to rate worker competence. Thirty-four percent of the workers were rated exceptionally competent. Forty-two percent were considered generally competent and 21% were rated as average. Only 3%, as might be expected, were rated as below average.

Worker's Perception of Service. Workers were asked to fill out a form indicating how they perceived the client's response to them.[5] Since not all workers were available, data are missing for 28% of the sample. The pattern of responses for those cases where the data were available indicated that the workers were most often confident that the mothers they had worked with at least felt free to talk to them (77%). In most cases, it was reported that the mother felt understood and liked by the worker (63%). Slightly fewer (59%) reported that the mothers saw them as a source of practical help. Fifty-seven percent thought that the mothers felt trusted by them. The smallest proportion of positive responses (48%) indicated that workers thought mothers perceived them as a source of emotional help in fewer than half the cases.

The same questions were asked in relation to the father. Although information about the father was, as noted, limited, it is clear that workers perceived the father's response as much more negative. Only 42% of the workers in 60 cases involving fathers thought he felt free to talk to them; 49% thought the fathers saw the workers as a source of practical help. Even fewer (36%) thought the fathers liked them, 34% thought that the fathers understood them, and 32% thought the fathers felt trusted by them. Only 28% thought they were perceived as a source of emotional help.

When workers were asked how much satisfaction they found in working with the study family, in 37% of the cases the workers felt generally satisfied. In the largest group (50%) of cases, workers expressed mixed feelings; in 13% they derived no satisfaction from working with the family in question. In 64% of the cases the workers thought the families had benefited as much as they could from the service. In 34% workers thought that the families might have benefited from more service than they had received.

Improvement. In reviewing the case material obtained from both the interview and case records, research staff made a series of seven judgments on problem areas and the extent to which they had or had not improved during the period covered. This was done primarily to ascertain that the time sequence of events in each case was clear. The areas were defined as the physical care of the children, their emotional care, economic problems, housing, marital relations, extended family, and community problems.

Given the nature of the study, it is evident that problems in the physical and/or emotional care of the children were reported in nearly all cases (88% and 89%, respectively) at intake. Economic problems were also reported in 72% of the cases, marital problems for 62% and housing problems for 60%. Only problems with the community (42%)

and with the extended family (39%) were reported in less than half the cases.

Again, given the nature of the services offered, it is not surprising that 77% of those who were described as having problems with the physical care of their children reported some improvement, as was the case with 75% of those reported as having problems with emotional care. Eighty-two percent of the families showed some improvement in at least one area other than child care, but no one problem area had more than a 50% improvement rate for those affected by it. Forty-seven percent of those who had housing problems showed some improvement in this area; the same held true for a third of those with economic, marital or community problems. The lowest improvement rate (18%) was for problems involving the extended family. Thus, while there may have been general improvement in the child-caring area and some positive effects may have carried over to other areas (or vice versa), the study families still appeared to be under considerable stress from sources other than childrearing.

A more specific method of assessing progress was to list indicators of improvement relating both to the parent and the child and ask the case reader to check the presence of evidence for each in the case reading schedule. Parallel lists were also included for indicators of failure. Of the 18 indicators of progress, derived from the literature, the median number of changes seen was four. The frequency with which the indicators were checked for parental behavior is shown in Table 3-4.

It may be noted that many of the indicators checked infrequently were related to improvement in childrearing practices. It is possible that workers record only gross changes in childrearing practices and are not aware of or do not record some of the subtler changes that may take place.

Of the list of new indicators that described positive changes in the child, a median of three were checked. Table 3-5 indicates the relative frequency of each form of improvement.

Table 3-4

Indicators of Parental Improvement

n=171

	%
Accepted removal of the children	27
Encouraged better school attendance	27
Removed abusive spouse	26
Developed insight into children's behavior	26
Improved economic conditions	19
Ability to express appropriate feelings	17
Ceasing abusive behavior	15
Increased ability to understand children's limitations	14
Seeing children in more positive light	13
Diminishing abusive behavior	9
Reduced demands of children	9
Being more affectionate	9
Reduced expectations of children	8
Ability to tolerate provocation	8
Use of nonphysical methods of punishment	7
Stopped assigning inappropriate responsibility	5
More aware of children's rights	4
Improved marital relations	1

Of the indicators of parental failure to change, the most commonly reported were the failure of the parent to show any insight into his or her own behavior (30%), resistance to referrals for help (25%), erratic handling of children (23%), and maintenance of low housekeeping standards (23%). In relation to the children, continuing emotional disturbances (19%), school failure (15%), learning disabilities (13%), and unmanageability (13%), were the indicators of failure most frequently checked.

Table 3-5
Improvements in the Child
n=571

	%
In good health	61
No significant emotional problems	49
Adequately dressed	46
Clean	44
Better nourished	39
Working at grade level or improving	34
Improved development	24
Relating better to parents	21
Relating better to siblings	19

Summary. Parents in the study sample were accused of neglect almost twice as frequently as they were accused of abuse. Nearly a third did not acknowledge that someone had complained and presented themselves as though they had initiated the request for service. Institutional settings such as social agencies were more likely to be sources of complaints than individuals. The sample was about evenly divided between families for whom there had been an earlier complaint and those for whom the complaint in question was the first. Seventy-five percent of the complaints were judged by the research staff to have apparent validity, while 25% remained in doubt. Less than a third of the families were involved in court action on the complaint itself.

Most of the respondents reported either a neutral or positive response to the workers and general acceptance and willingness to follow through on suggestions made. The most common action taken was an arrangement for foster care for the children involved.

Most families had more than one worker. The principal worker served a median of 16 months. The worker was usually female, under

35, and childless. She had a bachelor's degree, less than 3 years of experience in the protective services but often had some experience in other areas of child welfare.

The agencies had available a wide range of services. For two-thirds of the sample, the principal service was some form of relief from parental responsibility, such as placement in a foster care setting or with relatives. Children were placed for a median period of 12 months and most had returned home by the time of the interview.

Three-quarters of the families whose children remained at home were offered at least one form of service to supplement counseling by the worker, and more often were offered three or more. The analysis indicated that refusal of services was a more common problem than lack of available resources. Services related to material needs such as medical care, financial aid, and housing were most likely to be used. Refusal rates were highest for parent groups, mental hygiene services, and homemakers.

Respondents were most likely to have mixed feelings about the services given, rating some as helpful and others as not. Their overall response to protective service efforts was favorable in more than two-thirds of the cases.

Cases were active for a median of 2 years. Worker activity consisted heavily of home visits, and phone calls to families and other agencies. Home visits averaged about one a month. The quality of service was rated as good or very good for 55% of the families and as routine or poor for the remaining 45%. Three-quarters of the workers were rated as competent or exceptionally so by their supervisors. Workers indicated that they thought that mothers responded well to them but were not confident that they were seen as a source of help, particularly for emotional problems. They saw little positive response from the fathers they knew. Only a little over a third expressed satisfaction in working with the study families; most had mixed feelings. Two-thirds of the families were considered by the workers to have benefited from the service they received to the extent that they were capable of doing so.

Most families were judged to have shown some improvement in childrearing, but improvements in other problem areas were not common. Indicators of improvement in childrearing focused on physical care rather than on more subtle psychological changes.

Notes

1. The most recent available figures (in the 1977 Analysis of Child Abuse and Neglect Research, op. cit., pp. 9-10) indicate that most studies show a much higher ratio of neglect to abuse cases than was evident in this sample. This may be a reflection of the fact that the study concerns a serviced population. It is possible that abusive families remain under the surveillance of protective services agencies and draw more active attention from staff than the passive, neglectful families where the threat to the lives of the children is less direct. This may lead to the over-representation of abusive families in samples such as those required for studies concerned with service.

2. It is, of course, possible that both parent and agency versions of the source of the complaint are correct since there is often more than one source, i.e., a relative may report the apparent neglect of a child to the school teacher, who in turn reports it to the protective services agency. The record would identify the formal source of the report; the parent would be more likely to be conscious of an individual who might have "started it all."

3. Case aides were used in only one agency. They provided services that supplemented those of the case worker.

4. The worker assigned was usually but not always the major worker. Thus, this median is not the same as the one for the major worker reported earlier but is close to it.

5. This form was used in an earlier League project: A Second Chance for Families, by Jones, Neumann, and Shyne, CWLA, 1976.

Chapter IV

FACTORS ASSOCIATED WITH SUCCESSFUL OUTCOME

Chapters II and III indicated that the study sample of 171 families was predominantly female-headed, relatively young, large in size, and dependent on public funds or minimal earnings. Their recent histories were characterized by many forms of stress, particularly marital. The parents had multiple problems in rearing their children and mixed feelings about the satisfactions and responsibilities of parenthood. The complaints that initiated their contacts with protective services dealt heavily with neglect of a general nature. Most families reported a neutral or positive response to the interest of the protective services worker, as well as to the services offered. Most families accepted several services, the most common of which was placement of the child in the care of others, and were served for a median period of 2 years. Most of them were judged to have shown some improvement in childrearing but were less successful in other problem areas.

This general picture is based on data that also enabled the staff to analyze the relationships among variables describing the families and the services offered to them, and to identify the relationship between these variables and those that could be seen as indicators of improvement. As has been true in many such studies, the problem of defining an appropriate outcome variable was not readily overcome. This chapter discusses the problems and shows the influence of family and agency variables on the outcome variables that best served the study's purposes. Other outcome variables that proved inappropriate are discussed.

In developing the analysis, it became apparent that it is rarely possible to observe the actual "discontinuation" of abusive or neglectful behavior on the part of the parents. In research, as in practice, such changes must be inferred from specific indicators seen as reliable reflections of change. Furthermore, the problem of inadequate direct observation is confounded by the fact that society prohibits the indefinite continuation of abuse and neglect. Those abused or neglected children who are known to protective services are more likely than others to be removed from their homes and to remain in foster care as long as there is a likelihood that parents might resume their former behavior patterns. In reality then, changes for this population of parents are reflected in their ability to persuade their workers that they are capable of caring adequately for their children and refraining from abuse. The problem for this study was that of choosing valid indicators of such successful persuasion.

After considerable analytic exploration, only one measure--an index of improvement based largely on staff judgments--produced relatively unambiguous findings. Another outcome measure--the return of children from foster care--also proved useful but is obviously limited by the fact that it is applicable to only half the children in the sample. The findings produced through the use of these two outcome indicators will be presented, followed by a discussion of the problems presented by two other possible indicators: repeated complaints and case closing.

I. Overall Improvement

An index was developed that measured the overall improvement of the parents as reflected in both interview and case record data. It consisted of six strongly intercorrelated variables: 1) a research staff judgment as to whether there had been any improvement in the mother's physical care of the child; 2) a research staff judgment as to whether there had been any improvement in the mother's response to the child's emotional needs; 3) the number of indicators of parental progress (as described in Chapter III); 4) whether the case record gave indications of improvement in the mother's sense of adequacy as a mother; 5) whether there were indications in the record of improvement in the mother's self-esteem; 6) specific indications in the record of improvement in the mother's physical care of the child. Each respondent was assigned the mean value of these items as a score. The sample was then divided into three groups--those with poor outcome scores (30%), average scores (37%) or relatively high scores (33%).

Evidence of the predictive validity of this measure is provided by the fact that the score on the improvement index is correlated (.357) with the worker's feeling of satisfaction in working on the case: the greater the degree of improvement, the more likely the worker was to have expressed satisfaction in working on the case. The index is also correlated (.279) with the return of children from foster care.

Case Illustrations

To reduce some of the inevitable "dryness" of findings based on statistical analysis and give the reader a feeling for the kinds of families classified as low, average or high on improvement, the following case illustrations are presented as fairly typical.

Case I (Low Improvement.)

G. and S. were a white married couple, 44 and 41 years old respectively, parents of two daughters, aged 14 and 11, and two sons, aged 9 and 4. The father worked as a truck driver and the mother had returned to employment as a factory worker at the time of the interview. The case was open with the local protective services agency for 3½ years and had been closed a few months before the interview. It was opened on the complaint of a neighbor that the children were dirty and poorly clothed and that the mother had beaten them with a razor strap. The mother acknowledged that she had beaten her older son for breaking windows and that neighbors had complained that her house was not clean. The mother claimed that she was "nice" to each of the two workers who had been assigned to her but then "I got disgusted and told them to leave me alone."

The record indicated and the mother confirmed that she was offered counseling, specifically on financial management and homemaker service but refused both. The only service she accepted was the placement for adoption of an infant not fathered by her husband.

At the time of the interview, the parents appeared to be fairly comfortable economically but in need of better housing. They denied any significant problems with their children except for the eldest, who did not get along with her teachers and was behind in school. The case reader noted that the children were better clothed and fed than they were at the time of the initial complaint and that the parents were also encouraging better school attendance. The economic situation had improved because of the mother's employment. On the other hand, the parents showed no insight into their own behavior, resisted referrals for help, and had not improved with respect to housekeeping standards and money management.

Case II (Low Improvement.)

D., a white mother aged 48 and separated from the father of her children, has a 14-year-old daughter and two sons, aged 13 and 11. The case had been opened 2 years earlier, closed after 6 months of activity, and reopened again for a period of 2 months, with another department in the agency also active during the same period. The first complaint came from a mental hygiene clinic: bruises were observed on two of the children and the eldest had complained of beatings resulting from the mother's uncontrollable rages. The second complaint concerned the mother's lack of control over her children and the violent fights among them.

The mother was embarrassed by protective services' intervention but acknowledged that her daughter was extremely difficult to manage. She agreed to placement for two children. An initial short-term placement in a foster home was unsuccessful, and was followed by placement in a residential treatment center. The older boy was placed with the daughter but because they fought constantly, the children were discharged after 1 year. The daughter was placed in another center but the son remained at home. Mother has positive feelings about the two protective services workers she had known and saw their intervention as constructive. She rated the current placement of her daughter as a "very helpful" service but not so the placement of her son. Mother continued to be served directly by the mental hygiene clinic responsible for the initial referral but she was critical of the professional staff for their detachment and their lack of interest, saying she continued attendance only because her current worker was "a nice person to talk to."

The mother is currently on welfare. She had a 10th grade education, had worked at many unskilled jobs but now felt "too old and tired" to look for work or consider training. She had raised three children of a legal marriage, all in their mid-twenties and married, apparently with greater success than her second family, who were the children of a man with whom she had lived until her last pregnancy. She saw her mother and a sister but otherwise confined her social life to outings with her children. She continued to have major problems with her older son, but dealt more successfully with the younger one. She was one of the few parents who openly rejected the parental role for herself, saying that she was "not educated enough to deal with the job of childrearing."

The principal indications of progress checked were the mother's seeking for help in dealing with her children, her acceptance of their removal, her expression of appropriate feelings of anger, and some improvement in her relationship with the older children. There was no evidence of continuing abuse after the initial complaint. On the other hand, the indicators of failure included the absence of insight on the mother's part into her own behavior, taking foster care placement "a little too lightly," and the continuing severe emotional disturbance of the older children.

Case III (Average Improvement.)

M., a 25-year-old single white mother of a 4-year-old daughter and a 2-year-old son, was referred by a social agency on charges of neglect when the older child was 14 months old. The child was described as inadequately fed, very dirty and uncared for, and the home as "filthy." The mother ascribed the complaint to a jealous sister-in-law who was alleged to be trying to take the child away from her. M. was very suspicious of the protective services worker (the only one she had during the 2 years the case was active) from the beginning and remained so. She found him unhelpful and felt that he sided with her sister-in-law. M. claimed that she had refuted the latter's charges and that doctors had confirmed that her child was healthy. According to her, she had not been offered any services because the worker knew she had a homemaker through another agency. The case record indicated that she had been offered any number of services, some that proved unavailable, some that were accepted, and some resisted.

The mother described a number of sources of stress in her current situation. She was on welfare, was a chronic asthmatic, and was poorly housed. She had plans for vocational training but felt she could not carry them out until her son was older. She was socially isolated. Her daughter presented significant health problems but M. claimed she had no other difficulties with either child. She said she loved being a parent and had always felt that way. She denied any significant childhood problems other than those related to her health. At the time of the case closing, M. was seen as providing better physical and medical care for her children, who also showed no indications of emotional neglect. The housing situation, however, continued to be very poor. The worker felt that the mother had made no "real effort" to improve and that she continued to be fearful and suspicious despite considerable effort on the worker's part to reassure her and establish a more positive relationship.

Case IV (High Improvement.)

A., a white woman aged 38, separated from her husband, had two children living with her, a boy aged 14 and a daughter aged 12. She also had two grown sons (her first child was born when she was 14) and a daughter who had died. Three years earlier, a neighbor had complained to the protective services agency that the mother was an alcoholic who left her children with an elderly grandmother unable to supervise them. In A.'s account, she had requested placement of her younger children at the time of her elder daughter's death, when she felt too upset to care for them. A. had two workers and related particularly well to the second..

The mother underwent hospital treatment for alcoholism, and credited her recovery to this. The son was placed with an uncle, the daughter in an agency foster home. The former arrangement worked out well; the latter was less successful. Both placements had lasted for 2 years, when the children were returned to their mother. At the time of the interview, a court hearing was pending in which the agency was planning to recommend that the mother take custody permanently.

The mother had been on welfare for several years but had an interest in obtaining a high school equivalency diploma and becoming a nurse's aide. Her mother, whom she described as supportive, lived with her. A sister and a brother were also described as supportive. She had no problems with her daughter but she was troubled by her son's low level of school work. She was very conscious of the responsibilities of parenthood, and felt that she was better able to handle them since the agency's intervention.

The case record confirmed the picture of A. as a recovered alcoholic who had responded well to the foster care plan. Indicators of progress included seeking help for her own problems, insight into her own behavior, feeling generally more adequate, enhanced self-esteem, improved physical care of the children, and interest in better school performance. The children were in good health and adequately cared for. The daughter worked at grade level in school and was said to be much happier with the mother than in the foster home. No indicators of failure were checked.

Case V (High Improvement.)

R., aged 22, black, single, was the mother of two sons, aged 6 and 3, and a daughter, aged 5. Two years prior to the interview, R.'s brother had complained that she abused the youngest child. Medical examination did not substantiate this, but emotional and physical neglect were suspected. R. was aware of the complaint and angry about it. However, she had had four workers as of the time of the interview (case was still active), and found them all "lovely and helpful." All workers helped her with household management, arranging medical care, and encouraging her to attend a parent-child center. R. was on welfare, had never worked, but now had ambitions to be a nurse. She appeared heavily dependent on a brother and cut off from other members of the family. Her children presented a number of health problems, some quite serious, but she was getting appropriate help for them. She complained that her children fought a lot and that she had difficulty in managing them, but "thought it was great to be a parent." She felt she accepted the responsibilities of parenthood better than she had in the past and was more sure of herself.

The case record confirmed that R. was cooperative and responsive to offers of service. Indicators of progress were her ability to seek help, to share her concerns, and to understand her children's limitations. She was also more aware of their rights and showed greater ability to demonstrate affection. Her children were described as well cared for and receiving adequate medical care. The current worker also saw no indicators of failure to improve.

II. Factors Associated With Successful Outcomes

Three variables that describe the parent and two variables that describe the agency effort differentiate significantly between the parents who had shown improvement and those who had not. All of these variables account for a statistically significant proportion of the variance in improvement, independently of any interaction they may have had with other variables. Together, they account for 41% of the variance in improvement.

A. Variables Associated With Improvement

Characteristics associated with improvement are the mother's age, her competence as a housekeeper, and a tendency toward nonautoritarianism reflected in her willingness to demand less than total obedience from her children. The agency variables are the period of service and the number of services. Tables 4-1 through 4-5 illustrate each relationship.

1. <u>Mother's Age and Improvement</u>. Mothers who were 33 years of age or over were disproportionately represented among those who failed to improve.

2. <u>Mother's Housekeeping Ability and Improvement</u>. The case reading schedule called for an assessment of the mother's ability as a housekeeper, based on the information in the case record. Mothers rated as poor housekeepers also rated low on improvement; mothers rated average or high showed some or considerable improvement.

3. <u>Mother's Authoritarian Tendencies and Improvement</u>. As was indicated in Chapter 2, the self-administered questionnaire given the parents at the end of the interview included a number of items intended to measure authoritarian tendencies. These items were included to test the assumption that they differentiated between abusive and neglectful parents and that the more authoritarian parents would be less amenable to change. Of these items, only one differentiated between those parents who improved and those who did not: "Children should obey immediately when told to do something," a statement with which 70% of the respondents agreed. Parents who agreed <u>strongly</u> with this statement tended to have low improvement scores.

Table 4-1
Mother's Age and Improvement
n=171

	Under 28 n=73 %	29 - 32 n=35 %	33 and Over n=63 %
Low improvement	24	24	43
Average	37	34	37
High improvement	39	42	20
	100	100	100

Chi-square = 9.41, significant at .05 with 4 d.f.

Table 4-2
Housekeeping Ability and Improvement
n=158

	Poor Housekeeping n=50 %	Average or Better n=108 %
Low improvement	40	21
Average	36	39
Above average	24	40
	100	100

Chi-square = 6.92, significant at .05 with 2 d.f.

Table 4-3
Authoritarian Tendencies and Improvement
n=171

	Strong Agreement n=69 %	All Others n=102 %
Low improvement	41	23
Average	35	38
High improvement	25	39
	100	100

Chi-square = 7.24, significant at .027 with 2 d.f.

4. Period of Activity. The length of time a case was open was directly related to the degree of improvement seen. Families where little improvement was seen were those who were active a year or less. Cases active over 2 years tended to have an increasingly higher proportion of families showing improvement.

5. The Number of Services. The number of separate services given the families--other than counseling by protective services workers--varied from none to 11 with a median of three. The analysis indicated that those who received the average number were more likely to show some or a high rate of improvement than those who received either minimal or extensive service.

B. Factors Associated With Discharge From Foster Care

In 90 of the 171 families in the study (or 52% of the total), at least one of the children had been placed in foster care. All the children had returned home by the time of the discharge in 41% of the families. Some but not all had returned in 47%; none had returned in 12%. For this subsample, the return of the children could be seen as indicating that parents had persuaded the protective services agency that they could function as parents without abusing or neglecting their children. Thirty-four percent of the variance on return from foster care was accounted for in the analysis.

Apart from the association of discharge with general improvement, noted earlier in this chapter, two other variables were found to be associated with the return of children to their homes and accounted for statistically significant proportions of the variance on discharge, independently of overall improvement. The first is the number of children reared in the family; the larger the family, the greater the likelihood that at least some children in it will continue in foster care. (Table 4-6)

Another factor associated with discharge from foster care is income. This relationship misses statistical significance at the .05 level in cross-tabulation but accounts for 10% of the variance on discharge in

Table 4-4
Period of Activity and Improvement
n=171

	12 months or less n=27 %	13-18 n=29 %	19-24 n=30 %	25-31 n=35 %	32-36 n=21 %	37+ n=29 %
Little improvement	63	24	33	20	24	17
Some improvement	15	52	40	43	24	41
High improvement	22	24	27	37	52	42
	100	100	100	100	100	100

Chi-square = 25.30, significant at .005 with 10 d.f.

Table 4-5
Number of Services and Improvement
n=171

	3-4 Services n=60 %	All Others n=111 %
Low improvement	18	36
Some improvement	40	35
High improvement	42	29
	100	100

Chi-square = 6.26, significant at .04 with 2 d.f.

Table 4-6
Number of Children in Family and
Discharge from Foster Care
n=90

	1-2 Children n=29 %	3-4 Children n=36 %	5 or More n=25 %
Children at home	62	42	16
Children in care	38	58	84
	100	100	100

Chi-square = 11.77, significant at .003 with 2 d.f.

the regression analysis. Families whose incomes were above the median for this group were more likely to have their children returned home than those whose incomes were below the median. (Table 4-7)

It should be noted that, since many of the subjects of the study were on welfare, the trend observed in Table 4-7 could be an artifact of the welfare system in which allowances are reduced when children are placed away from home. A review of the interview material indicated that such reductions did occur in some of the welfare cases involved, but in the majority such reductions were not made or the family was not on welfare.

III. Dubious Outcome Variables

Researchers generally focus their reports on their strongest findings and do not, as a rule, burden their readers with discussions of analytic procedures that proved unproductive. In this instance, however, the results of some of the study's efforts merit reporting, because they may contribute to knowledge of how not to assess child abuse or neglect. The strong concern in the field with the problem of establishing the true incidence of abuse and neglect in this country means in turn that the identification of variables that are valid indicators of the extent to which the reported cases are true cases of abuse or neglect is of central importance. Valid indicators make it possible to assess not only the

Table 4-7

Income and Return from Foster Care

n=90

	Below Median n=51 %	Median or Higher n=39 %
Children at home	33	51
Children in care	67	49
	100	100

Chi-square = 2.94, significant at .09 with 1 d.f.

magnitude of a problem but the extent and the conditions under which positive change is effected as well. Some indicators assumed to be valid on a common sense basis prove on closer examination to have less validity than had been thought, as was the case in this study.

A. Multiple Complaints

Studies of changes in the behavior of abusive or neglectful parents have been referred to in some quarters as studies in "recidivism." Data from the present study suggest that this is a questionable concept for use in analysis of this problem. The dictionary defintion of "recidivism" is a "tendency to relapse into a previous condition or mode of behavior." It has also been customary in some fields of practice to limit the meaning of the term to relapses after treatment. In either case, the term might be appropriate for studies limited to the physical abuse of children where the parent's behavior is likely to be episodic. The majority of the parents in this study were neglectful, which means primarily that they failed to take actions concerning the health and welfare of their children that are generally considered essential. This is a condition of passivity rather than action, one that is usually chronic and for which "recidivism" is not an appropriate term. The number of complaints may be a function of the relative visibility of some families' problems rather than of any actual changes in parental behavior. For instance, the same pattern may be observed and reported by different teachers, neighbors, social workers, etc., at different times and under different conditions.

In the sample studied, slightly less than half (48%) were involved in only one complaint. For 24%, there had been complaints prior to the 1973 complaint on which inclusion in the study was based. For 18% there were complaints after 1973 and for 5% complaints both before and after. An analysis using multiple complaints as the dependent variable was carried out.

When families in which there were multiple complaints were compared with families in which there was only one complaint, relatively few significant differences appeared. There were no differences between these two groups in their scores on the improvement index, our principal outcome variable. The significant differences that were identified tend to support the hypothesis that repeated complaints are a function of the family's visibility.

1. <u>Multiple Complaints and Repetition of Life Style</u>. As noted in Chapter II, a list of ongoing stresses used in the form developed by the National Clearinghouse on Child Neglect and Abuse was incorporated in the case reading schedule. One of these stresses was listed as "repetition of life style," referring to a long-term pattern of deviant behavior. Families showing this form of stress had a history of severe problems usually dating from the childhood of one or both parents, continuing into adulthood and predating any evidence of abuse or neglect. This type of stress was identified in 33% of the families in the study and was strongly associated with multiple complaints, as Table 4-8 indicates. It also accounts for 6% of the variance on repeated complaints, much more than any other related variable.

2. <u>Size of Family and Multiple Complaints</u>. A second influential variable in relation to multiple complaints is the number of children reared in the family. As Table 4-9 indicates, one-child families were seldom involved in more than one complaint. The proportion rises sharply with the two-child family, levels off for three to five children, then rises sharply again for those families with six or more children.

3. <u>Multiple Complaints and Client Accessibility</u>. The analysis indicated that the parents' attitudes (positive or negative) toward their principal workers, and their initial perception of the services offered (whether seen as a threat or a form of help), were highly correlated with their responses to four statements on the self-administered questionnaire:[1]

> Social workers give you a chance to talk about the things that are on your mind.

> Social workers tell you where to go to get the things you need.

> Agencies act like parents have no rights at all--they think they own the children.

Table 4-8

Repetition of Life Style and
Multiple Complaints

n=171

	No "Repetition of Life Style" n=114 %	"Repetition of Life Style" n=57 %
Single complaint	59	33
Multiple complaints	41	67
	100	100

Chi-square = 9.83, significant at .002.

Table 4-9

Size of Family and Multiple Complaints

n=171

	One n=19 %	Two n=34 %	Three n=45 %	Four n=25 %	Five n=25 %	Six or More n=23 %
Multiple complaints	26	53	42	44	56	78
Single complaint	74	47	58	56	44	22
	100	100	100	100	100	100

Chi-square = 13.53, significant at .02 with 5 d.f.

Social workers talk too much and never really listen to you.

Taken together, responses on these items could be seen as reflections of the client's accessibility to service. Those who expressed positive feelings about their workers saw the offer of service as a form of help, and agreed with the first two statements that were listed. They disagreed with the second pair and were relatively accessible to their workers, in contrast to those who responded in the opposite direction. Parents whose scores were low or average on this index of

Table 4-10
Client Accessibility and Multiple Complaints
n=171

	Low Accessibility n=59 %	Average Accessibility n=58 %	High Accessibility n-54 %
Multiple complaints	59	53	35
Single complaint	41	47	65
	100	100	100

Chi-square = 7.06, significant at .03 with 2 d.f.

accessibility were more likely to fall into the multiple complaint group; those with high scores were more likely to be among those involved in a single complaint. (Table 4-10)

Since the measure of accessibility was made after the complaint, it is impossible to be certain of the direction of this relationship. If the measure represents a relatively stable attitude on the part of the respondent, it is possible that the absence of response or lack of accessibility to workers' efforts at the time of the initial complaint helped create the conditions that made the second complaint possible. On the other hand, it is equally likely that those families about whom more than one complaint was made became inaccessible to agency help as a result of greater exposure to agencies, rather than having been inaccessible to begin with.

Large families in general and those with long-standing multiple problems in particular tend to be highly visible in any community, even in slum areas where they are not uncommon. They are more exposed to a variety of welfare workers, health personnel, and teachers. It is to be expected that such visibility will lead to repeated complaints. Conversely, the absence of repeated complaints may not signify improvement; it may only mean that abusive or neglectful behavior on the part of smaller families with a less obtrusive life style is less visible.

B. Case Closing

Theoretically, the closing of a neglect or an abuse case in a protective services department for a family where the children are in the home should signify, in most instances, that the parents have convinced the authorities that they are no longer abusive or neglectful. If this is so, the status of the case should be an appropriate indicator of successful outcome. In this study, however, the correlational analysis indicated that positive change was related to continuing case activity rather than to closing; the greater the number of improvements or indicators of progress, the more likely the case was to be open rather than to be closed. This is a relationship that might be expected in an agency where client cooperation is voluntary and where an early closing often means resistance or lack of response. That this should also be the case in a protective services setting is surprising. An analysis of the relationship between key independent variables and the status of the case also provided further evidence that there are many variables that influence case closing, besides positive changes in the family situation, that serve to cancel out the impact of improvement.

For the purpose of this analysis, the sample was separated into two subsamples: families who received inhome services only and those whose children were placed in foster care at some time during the period covered. Analysis indicated that a number of strong differences between these two groups affecting the status of the cases justified treating them separately. Foster care cases were significantly more likely to have been active more than 2 years (58%) than the inhome cases (40%). They were more likely to involve single parents (77%) than the inhome group (58%). The presence of chronic health problems in the mother was much greater in the foster care sample (38%) than in the inhome group (12%). The foster care group was more likely to have been referred for mental hygiene services (37% compared to 21%), and to have had a history of earlier complaints (31% to 19%). Agency variables also differed for the two groups. The inhome group was more

81

likely to have had workers with low caseloads (42%), compared to 22% for the foster care sample. Workers who had caseloads limited to abuse and neglect were more likely to have children in foster care than those with general child welfare caseloads.

For the 81 families who received inhome support service, case closing was associated with a relatively short period of service--less than 2 years. Associated with this shorter time period was the involvement of only one worker who offered relatively few services. On an index that reflected the degree to which the worker found the family accessible and responsive, the analysis indicated that most families in closed cases in this group had been found relatively inaccessible.

Other differences between active and closed inhome cases were related to family characteristics. Families who were free of housing problems were more likely to be in the closed category; families with housing problems were more likely to be active. Mothers who were rated average or better as housekeepers were more likely to be in the closed group than among the active cases. Mothers who refrained from using physical punishment were more likely to be in the closed category than those who used this method of discipline.

When one looks at the sample of 90 families whose children were placed in foster care, one finds that among the active cases, 55% were served by one worker for over a year and a half. The large majority of the closed cases (79%) had only one worker, regardless of the period of activity. The behavior of the major worker was more likely to have been seen as positive in the closed cases than in the active cases. The approach of the worker was more likely to be seen as authoritarian in the active cases than in the closed cases. Closed cases were more often found in agencies with relatively low proportions of trained workers than those with a higher proportion of trained workers.

Only two client characteristics were related to the status of foster care cases. The presence of housing problems, as with inhome cases, was related to continued activity. Cases of parents who rejected the parental role were more likely to be active; cases of more accepting parents tended to be closed.

In general then, the picture is one in which positive forces (acceptance of parental role, absence of housing problems, mother's capacity as a housekeeper, avoidance of physical punishment) that work toward case closing are offset by other more negative forces that also lead to case closing (initial inaccessibility or unresponsiveness to workers, untrained workers). This phenomenon, in turn, suggests that the status of the case, like the repeated complaint, is not a sound indicator of the discontinuation of abusive or neglectful behavior on the part of parents.

IV. Negative Findings

In the discussion of a problem about which there is great concern and speculation, with a rapidly developing practice mythology, negative findings--areas in which no differences are found--may have as much, if not more, substantive significance than positive findings. In this study, the examination of the relationship between the various outcomes and variables describing both the family and the community were by no means limited to those reported in the preceding sections. The absence of a relationship with any form of improvement is worth noting on a number of variables.

No relationship was found between any type of improvement and the type of case, i.e., whether the parent was abusive or neglectful. Nor was there any relationship between improvement and any specific form of stress suffered by the parent, other than the "life style" category noted earlier. Apart from income, no other socioeconomic variable (welfare status, housing, type of employment) bore any relationship to improvement. Nonwhite parents had the same rate of improvement as white parents.

The type of family did not differentiate between those who improved and those who did not; families that included both parents did not have a better improvement rate than those headed by mothers alone. There was no relationship to the parent's attitude toward the parenting role; parents with mixed feelings had the same improvement rate as those who were more accepting. None of the data we were able to obtain on actual childrearing practices (in contrast to the attitudinal variable noted in 4-3) differentiated between those who improved and those who did not. Neither did measures of self-esteem. Despite strong tendencies toward social isolation in the study sample, this variable also did not distinguish between those who improved and those who did not. Neither the parents' descriptions of their childhood nor history of physical abuse or neglect differentiated between their scores on the improvement measure.

There was no significant variation in the improvement rate among the six cooperating agencies, despite regional differences and variations in size, structure, and staffing. Worker training and experience had no relation to the improvement measure, nor did the number of workers on the case, court involvement, the time and effort made by the worker, or whether the worker was authoritative or supportive in her approach to the family. The extent to which families appeared accessible to help from social workers did not necessarily predict a good or bad outcome.

V. Summary and Conclusions

The key findings of this study indicate that the factors most strongly associated with the apparent discontinuation of abusive or neglectful behavior on the part of the parents are the mother's age, her housekeeping ability, nonauthoritarian attitudes, a relatively long period of agency activity and a moderate number of services in addition to counseling.

Of these, the relationship with age is perhaps the least surprising finding; younger mothers are apparently more open to change, have more resources, and are more receptive to help. The relationship with housekeeping ability is also not surprising but its interpretation may vary. At one time, this relationship would have been seen--and still might be seen in some quarters--as evidence of middle class bias on the part of social workers, that is, a predisposition to favor clients who share with the worker values such as cleanliness and orderliness, despite the fact that they are not necessarily related to the capacity to raise children. In light of what has been said earlier about the problem of observing changes in childrearing behavior, the significance of house-keeping ability for the worker may lie largely in its visibility. If the mother is sufficiently organized to keep house at an adequate level, it may be inferred that she is also feeding and clothing her children adequately, as well as seeing to their school and health needs. Another possible interpretation is that the mother has learned to "role-play" the adequate parent and has perceived better housekeeping as one of its requirements. Some of the mother's childrearing practices may still be dubious and workers may have strong suspicions that emotional neglect continues to be a problem, but as long as there is physical evidence of competence, there is little pressure to continue protective service intervention.

That personality variables or childrearing attitudes may show some relationship to improvement is indicated by the link between the measure of authoritarianism and the improvement index. The fact that this relationship was noted on only a single measure suggests that either such variables are not strong factors in improvement or that such an assessment requires a greater variety of instruments than it was possible to develop in this study. The fact that the measure of authoritarianism was taken after parental behavior improved also suggests a learned response resulting from intervention rather than a personality trait or attitude that existed before the change in behavior and helped to induce it.

The role of length of service in association with improvement suggests that there are few spontaneous or quick recoveries for parents who have been abusive or neglectful. The link between the average number of services and improvement indicates, on the one hand, that worker counseling in and of itself is insufficient to bring about change for these families. On the other hand, it also indicates that the chances for improvement level off after a certain degree of involvement in other services is reached. An exceptionally high number of referrals for service may reflect the "shopping around" phenomenon in which family involvement with agencies is superficial and has no real impact. It may also mean that cases requiring an unusually high number of services present such a multiplicity of problems that they defy all efforts toward improvement.   Thus, the agency factors most relevant to parental improvement are the ability to sustain services for a period of at least 2 years and the choice of three or four concrete services that support the worker's efforts. Other service factors--the frequency of contact, the stability of the workers, their education or experience--do not apparently carry the same weight.

In cases where the child's return from foster care can be used as an outcome measure, the associated factors are the small size of the family and the adequacy of its income. Again, the evidence indicates that personality factors do not play a significant role and that parents' ability to persuade agencies of their ability to care for their children is more likely to be related to the economic burdens they carry.

The findings also indicate that neither repeated complaints nor the status of the case with the agency, whether it was active or closed, are valid indicators of change.

Note

1.   These measures were developed by the Family Welfare Research Program of the Columbia University School of Social Work and are reported in Shirley Jenkins and Elaine Norman, Final Deprivation and Foster Care. New York: Columbia University Press, 1972, p. 154.

Chapter V
DIFFERENCES BETWEEN ABUSIVE, NEGLECTFUL, AND MARGINAL PARENTS

Chapter IV focused on those findings that answered the questions for which the study was funded, to the extent that the available data permitted tentative conclusions.   However, like most studies based on indepth interviews, the quantity of data collected permitted the research staff to explore some problems that, while not directly related to the study's central questions, are of interest to the field in general and merit presentation. In this chapter, we look first at the differences among the types of parent served and then at the differences in agency response to these parents.

I. Differences Between Abusive, Neglectful, and Marginal Families
The survey of the literature made in preparation for this study indicated a general tendency in the field to regard abuse and neglect as different phenomena, representing different personality problems, each with its own etiology.[1] In the course of the analysis, the question of the extent to which the abusive and neglectful parents had different characteristics was examined.

The presence of conflicting or ambiguous evidence in a number of cases made it necessary to base the classification of the cases on a staff judgment rather than on the complaint itself, as described in the case record or by the respondent. As a result, the sample was divided into three categories: 1) neglect (convincing evidence of neglect in both the record and the interview); 2) abuse (convincing evidence of abuse in both the record and the interview); 3) marginal (evidence of abuse or neglect from either source was not wholly convincing). The first category covered 48% of the sample; the latter two, 27% and 25% respectively. Cases where both abuse and neglect were involved were classified as "abuse." All variables on which differences might have been expected were cross-tabulated against these three categories.

Fifteen statistically significant differences related to family characteristics were identified. The first five tables that follow show how the abusive families differed from the others. The next seven show differences in the neglecting families, and the following three show differences in the marginal families. In addition, eight statistically significant differences were found in the ways in which these families were handled by the agencies involved. Some of these differences became apparent in the analysis of the larger sample of children but were not seen in the analysis of the family sample.

A. Abusive Families

1. Table 5-1 indicates that fathers are more likely to figure in abuse cases as the perpetrator than in either of the other types. In neglect cases, the mother or both parents are more likely to be named as the perpetrators, and this is even more likely to be true among the marginal cases.

2. Table 5-2 shows abusive families were less likely than either the marginal or the neglectful families to be seen as carrying unusually heavy childrearing burdens (many children, close spacing, severe child health problems).

3. The proportion of parents who reported experiencing excessive restrictions and harsh treatment as children was considerably higher for abusive parents than for the rest of the sample.[2] (Table 5-3) For example, one of these respondents said that because she was conceived

Table 5-1
Perpetrator and Type of Case
n=162

	Abuse n=42 %	Neglect n=81 %	Marginal n=39 %
Mother	48	57	74
Father	45	5	3
Both parents	7	38	23
	100	100	100

Chi-square = 48.41 with 4 d.f. Significant at .001

Table 5-2
Childrearing Burdens and Type of Case
n=171

	Abuse n=46 %	All Others n=125 %
Heavy childrearing burdens	30	51
Not heavy	70	49
	100	100

Chi-square = 5.03 with 1 d.f. Significant at .02

Table 5-3
Excessive Childhood Restrictions and Type of Case
n=171

	Abuse n=46 %	Neglect n=83 %	Marginal n=42 %
Excessive restrictions	35	13	19
Not excessive	65	87	81
	100	100	100

Chi-square = 8.49 with 2 d.f. Significant at .01

out of wedlock while her mother's husband was away, she was always rejected by him and, among other things, was not allowed to sleep in the house with the rest of the family but was given a room on the outside. Another described having been reared, while her mother worked, by a very strict grandmother who held puritanical views of sex, regarding all men as "dirty." Another was sexually abused. Still another said, "My place was in the home looking after the younger children." One said her parents were stern and didn't let her go out much. Three others said their parents were "too strict and punished too much" or watched them too closely. Another reported being disciplined by being forced to stay in the house. Another said she had to ask permission to go anywhere and that she was given chores to do but never an allowance. Another said her father did not allow her to go to parties. Half of these respondents also reported the use of physical punishment and, in many instances, the punishment was frequent and severe. However, the dominant characteristic of the childhood experiences of these respondents seems to have been an atmosphere of harshness and an absence of warmth, whether or not physical punishment was used and regardless of how accepting they may have been of the parental attitudes toward discipline. It is noteworthy that it is this variable that distinguished between the abusive parents and the others, not the use of physical punishment itself.

4. In looking at the sample of children involved in these complaints, the analysis indicated that major problems in parent-child relations at the time of the interview tended to be reported more frequently for abuse victims than for neglect victims. (Table 5-4) The parents of abuse victims were also more likely to express concern about relationship problems with their children than were the parents of neglect victims.[3] (Table 5-5)

A review of abuse cases in which relationship problems continued to be serious despite the apparent diminution or discontinuance of abuse showed that some involved problems emanating from fear on the part of

Table 5-4
Problems With Parents and Type of Case
n=354*

	Abuse Victims n=98 %	Neglect Victims n=256 %
Current problems	29	13
No problems reported	71	87
	100	100

Chi-square = 10.43 with 1 d.f. Significant at .01

Table 5-5
Parental Attitudes Toward Relationship Problems
and Type of Case
n=326*

	Abuse Victims n=87 %	Neglect Victims n=239 %
Concerned	51	26
Not concerned	49	74
	100	100

Chi-square = 16.53 with 1 d.f. Significant at .001

*In the child sample, 134 children were the siblings of victims. The remaining cases in the total sample of 571 were those in which information was missing. In both situations there were no differences in relation to siblings.

the children of a father who had been abusive and from whom the mother was trying to protect them. In most instances, however, the problems described involved some very provocative behavior, lending support to the now increasingly common observation that child abuse victims are not necessarily passive recipients of parental violence but are involved in a circular process in which they often provoke the parent's response.[4]   Some of the following descriptions illustrate the point:

A 6-year-old girl whose father is the abusing parent. He gets frustrated when she doesn't listen. She has a very short attention span and is stubborn.

A 7-year-old boy who "mouths off" and a 4-year-old girl who "cries too much and wants her own way" (both in same family).

A 6-year-old boy who is described as so hyperactive he needs to be in a special school.

A 12-year-old boy whom mother describes as "taking on a dumb attitude, does not listen, lies, and is defiant." She tries to talk to him but "if he is really into a violent act, she goes after him and shakes him."

A 14-year-old boy who is "a hyperactive, acting out, delinquent, who cannot abide by the rules," and had to be placed in foster care.

A 6-year-old boy who will, in relation to both the parents and other significant adults, "push people to the limit to see how much he can get away with." Mother says he whines so much that she would like to "get a muzzle and put it on him."

A 6-year-old girl who is described as "uncontrollable, belligerent, defiant" and a problem in school.

B. Neglectful Families

1. Among the evaluations made by research staff in reviewing the interview and case record data was one involving the overall stress under which the parents in the sample appeared to be trying to function. This referred to stress in general, based on economic, housing, health or other problems, not childrearing alone. In the analysis, parents charged with neglect were more likely than others to be evaluated as being under exceptionally heavy stress. (Table 5-6)

Table 5-6

Heavy Stress and Type of Case

n=171

	Neglect n=83 %	All Others n=88 %
Heavy stress	32	17
Moderate or little stress	68	83
	100	100

Chi-square = 4.72 with 1 d.f. Significant at .05.

2. References were made in Chapter IV to the apparently greater visibility in the community of neglectful families. This inference is supported by an analysis indicating that these families were more likely to have had problems with the community at the time of intake (complaints and conflicts with neighbors, landlords, etc.) than either of the other categories of parents. (Table 5-7)

Table 5-7

Community Problems at Intake and Type of Case

n=171

	Neglect n=83 %	Abuse n=46 %	Marginal n=42 %
Community problem	57	33	33
No community problem	43	67	67
	100	100	100

Chi-square = 9.69 with 2 d.f. Significant at .008

3. Neglectful families were also more likely to have presented housing problems at intake than either the abusive or the marginal families. (Table 5-8)

Table 5-8
Housing Problems at Intake and Type of Case
n=171

	Neglect n=83 %	Abuse n=46 %	Marginal n=42 %
Housing problem	74	50	43
No housing problem	26	50	57
	100	100	100

Chi-square = 7.99 with 2 d.f. Significant at .02

4. Alcoholism, another item on the list of stresses derived from the National Clearinghouse Form, was nearly twice as likely to be checked as a form of stress for families against whom complaints of neglect were made as was the case for either the abusive or the marginal families.[5] (Table 5-9)

Table 5-9
Alcoholism and Type of Case
n=171

	Neglect n=83 %	Abuse n=46 %	Marginal n=42 %
Alcoholism present	48	26	21
Alcoholism not present	52	74	79
	100	100	100

Chi-square = 11.22 with 2 d.f. Significant at.004

5. In reviewing the indicators of progress described in the record, it was noted that children who were neglect victims showed improvements in health more frequently than either abuse victims or the siblings of victims. (Table 5-10)

Table 5-10

Improvements in Health and Type of Case

n=552 children

	Neglect Victims n=289 %	All Others n=263 %
Improvements in health	61	50
No improvements indicated	39	50
	100	100

Chi-square = 6.44 with 1 d f.   Significant at .02

6. Neglect victims had fewer relationship problems with parents than did abuse victims, as Table 5-4 indicated, but those who had them were more likely to show improvement. (Table 5-11)

Table 5-11

Improvements in Relationship With Parents and Type of Case

n=172 children*

	Abuse n=65 %	Neglect n=107 %
Major problems/no improvement	32	26
Minor problems/no improvement	60	45
Improvement	8	29
	100	100

Chi-square = 12.92 with 2 d.f.   Significant at .01

*No differences were seen in relation to siblings.

7. On the other hand, neglect victims were more likely to have a higher incidence of school problems, as reflected in the indicators of school failure, than were other children in the sample. (Table 5-12)

Table 5-12
School Failures and Type of Case
n=552 children

	Neglect Victims n=289 %	Abuse Victims n=110 %	Siblings of Neglect Victims n=82 %	Siblings of Abuse Victims n=71 %
Continuing school problems	16	9	10	4
No school problems	84	91	90	96
	100	100	100	100

Chi-square = 10.82 with 3 d.f. Significant at .01

C. Marginal Families

1. Marginal families differed by race and by family structure from those who were more clearly abusive or neglectful. The proportion of white families among those whose cases were judged "marginal" was considerably higher than for the rest of the sample. (Table 5-13)

Table 5-13
Race and Type of Case
n=171

	Marginal n=42 %	Neglect n=83 %	Abuse n=46 %
White	86	65	67
Nonwhite	14	35	33
	100	100	100

Chi-square = 6.09 with 2 d.f. Significant at .05

The relationship between marginal status and race may be spurious, stemming from the association of both with marital status.

Only 6% of the nonwhite families in the study were married, in contrast to 27% for the entire sample. Among the nonwhite families, the father was more likely to have left the scene before the family became active with protective services, so that the custody battle syndrome occurred less often or not at all. It is also possible that among poverty-level minorities, a degree of neglect or even abuse is "expected" behavior, so that only the more extreme cases where the evidence is strongest are likely to reach the agency.

2. Marginal families were much more likely to be two-parent families than were those for whom the evidence for either abuse or neglect was convincing. (Table 5-14)

Table 5-14

Family Structure and Type of Case

n=171

	Marginal n=42 %	Neglectful n=83 %	Abusive n=46 %
Two-parent	48	27	28
Single-parent	52	73	72
	100	100	100

Chi-square = 6.13 with 2 d.f.   Significant at .05

3. Similarly, the marginal families also presented a more stable marital picture than the other families. (Table 5-15)

On the surface, the relationship with family status suggests that the "marginal" families were, as might have been expected, relatively more stable than those where the charges of abuse and neglect were either admitted or borne out by the evidence. A review of the cases involved, however, reveals that there is more than one explanation for this relationship. As was expected, the largest group of cases classed as "marginal" were so coded because the complaint involved a single episode, where the evidence of either abuse or neglect was not clear-

Table 5-15

Marital Stability and Type of Case

n=171

	Marginal n=42 %	All Others n=129 %
No changes	64	42
Changes*	36	58
	100	100

Chi-square = 5.11 with 1 d.f. Significant at .02

*Separation, divorce, or remarriage within the period covered by the interview.

cut, or where services were given for preventive reasons. However, about a quarter of the group of families were so classified because of a very unstable marital situation itself. The parents involved were engaged in custody battles or other conflicts in which charges and countercharges were made, usually about the mother's capacity to care for her children. These families were classified as marginal in relation to the abuse/neglect complaint because it was impossible to ascertain from the evidence available how much substance, if any, there was to the charges made by one parent against the other. In the emotionally charged atmosphere it was evident that the charges could be overstated by the attacking parent and understated by the one on the defensive.

II. Differences in the Handling of Abuse, Neglect, and Marginal Cases

Some significant differences found in this analysis lay not in the families themselves but in the ways in which their cases were handled by the protective service agencies. Some of these differences have to do with the use of placement, others with more general aspects of agency activity.

A. Use of Placement

1. Children in marginal families were unlikely to be placed in foster care. One might have anticipated that families charged with abuse would be more vulnerable to having their children removed than those charged with neglect but, as Table 5-16 indicates, this was not so for this sample.

Table 5-16

Placement and Type of Case

n=169

	Marginal n=42 %	Neglect n=82 %	Abuse n=45 %
No placement	60	32	33
Foster home placement	29	38	40
Other placement	11	30	27
	100	100	100

Chi-square = 10.87 with 4 d.f. Significant at .03

2. Table 5-17 indicates that abuse victims, if placed, were more likely to have multiple placements than either neglect victims or their siblings.

Table 5-17

Stability of Placement and Type of Placement

n=185

	Neglect Victims n=110 %	Abuse Victims n=52 %	Siblings of Victims n=23 %
One placement	76	52	78
Two or more	24	48	22
	100	100	100

Chi-square = 10.90 with 2 d.f. Significant at .01

3. Two other differences in relation to placement were noted that just missed statistical significance at the .05 level and so must be evaluated more cautiously. An examination of the sample of 212 children who were placed indicated that institutional placements were more likely to be used for abuse victims (30%), and foster homes were more likely (58%) to be used for victims of neglect. Day care was also more likely to be used for neglect victims than for abuse victims (22% compared to 6%). There may be a tendency in the direction of a complete separation for abuse victims as compared to neglect victims, but it is not as strong as might be expected when one considers the relatively greater public and professional concern for the abuse victim.

Another relationship that just misses statistical significance is that between the type of complaint and the attitude toward placement. Of the 106 families in which placement was proposed, although not necessarily implemented, parents charged with abuse were somewhat more likely to resist the suggestion (73%) than were the parents considered neglectful (52%) or those classed as marginal (42%).

B. Other Differences in Handling

1. Not surprisingly, the marginal cases were much more likely to be closed in less than 18 months than either abuse or neglect cases. Neglect cases were most likely to be active between 19 and 31 months. The periods of service given abuse cases were almost evenly distributed among the three time categories into which the sample was divided. (Table 5-18)

2. It will also come as no surprise that families where a complaint of abuse was made were much more likely to be involved in court hearings than either neglectful or marginal families. Those charged with neglect were slightly more likely to be involved with the court (22%) than the marginal families (14%), but the difference is much stronger for those charged with abuse. (Table 5-19)

Table 5-18

Period of Activity and Type of Case

n=171

	Marginal n=42 %	Neglect n=83 %	Abuse n=46 %
18 months or less	50	23	34
19-31 months	26	47	33
32 months or more	24	30	33
	100	100	100

Chi-square = 10.62 with 4 d.f. Significant at .05

Table 5-19

Court Hearings and Type of Case

n=171

	Abuse n=46 %	All Others n=125 %
Court hearing	54	19
No court hearing	46	81
	100	100

Chi-square = 18.64 with 1 d.f. Significant at .001

3. Another difference, which is more difficult to explain than the others, is that families charged with abuse were more likely to have had workers with high case loads, the neglect cases were more likely to have workers with above average loads, while the marginal families were more likely distributed among all workers. Since the proportion of cases of each type did not vary by agency, this difference cannot be explained by differences in agency case load size. (Table 5-20)

Table 5-20

Size of Case Load and Type of Case

n=171

	High Case Loads n=30 %	Above Average n=41 %	Average n=56 %	Low Case Loads n=44 %
Marginal cases	23	17	27	30
Neglect cases	30	68	48	43
Abuse cases	47	15	25	27
	100	100	100	100

Chi-square = 13.92 with 6 d.f. Significant at .03

It is possible that this relationship may be a function of the greater urgency felt in dealing with abuse cases and neglect cases that may result in their assignment to workers who are already overloaded.

III. Negative Findings

As was the case with our key findings, some negative findings take on significance, especially when they run counter to expectations or to differences seen elsewhere. In relation to client characteristics, neither the mother's age nor the number of children she had differentiated between the marginal, the abusive, and the neglectful. Nor did any measure reflecting the family's socioeconomic status. Nor did church affiliation. None of these groups was significantly more isolated than the others.[6] The mother's health made no difference: an abusive mother was not likely to be seen as more seriously disturbed than a neglectful or marginal mother. Although one might have expected the neglectful mothers to be the poorest housekeepers, in fact the three groups did not vary either in the interviewers' assessments or in the data based on case records. Also, somewhat surprisingly, the "life style" stress, mentioned in Chapter IV, was not necessarily more characteristic of the neglectful mothers than of the others. Neither the abusive nor neglectful parents were more rejecting in their attitude toward the parental role than were the marginal parents. Nor did the degree of self-esteem vary.

Although the literature describes abusive parents in particular as suspicious and hard to reach, those who were respondents in the study were just as likely as the others to be considered reliable respondents, and, except for the tendency of abusive parents to resist foster care placement, there was little difference in their responsiveness to the agency or its workers. As was noted in Chapter IV, they did not vary in the extent to which they improved by the outcome measures used.

From the standpoint of agency activity, it is noteworthy that the worker's approach (whether authoritarian or supportive) did not vary with the type of complaint nor was there any difference in the training or experience of workers assigned, the quality of service given (other than case load size), or the investment of effort made.

Summary

Evidence was found in this study of significant differences between families who abused children, those who neglected them, and those who were suspected of tendencies in either direction. Among abusive families, the father was more likely to be the perpetrator. The family's childrearing burdens were not as heavy as those of other families. Abusive mothers were more likely to have experienced harsh treatment or excessive restrictions as children. They reported more problems and more concern about these problems than other families.

Neglectful families were judged to be under heavier external stress than others. They were more likely to have had community or housing problems at intake and alcoholism was found more frequently among them. Neglect victims had fewer relationship problems with their parents but those who had them were more likely to improve. However, they had a higher incidence of school problems.

Marginal families were more likely to be white, to include both parents, and to have undergone fewer marital changes during the period covered.

Differences in agency handling of these types of parent were also evident. Children in marginal families were unlikely to be placed in foster care. Abused children were more likely to have multiple placements. Marginal families were more likely to have their cases closed in less than 18 months. Cases involving abuse were more likely to be heard in court and were more likely to be assigned to workers with high case loads.

No demographic or socioeconomic factors differentiated among the three groups, nor did any measure of attitudes toward parenting or toward services.

Notes and References

1. Evidence on this point is also seen in more recent studies: Milton Kotelchuck, op. cit., pp. 14-35; Arthur H. Green, M.D., "The Psychological Effects of Child Abuse and Neglect" (photocopy), 1973, pp. 18-19.

2. This is similar to Kotelchuck's finding (op. cit., p. 16) that mothers of abused children had a more unhappy childhood than mothers involved in other varieties of pediatric social illness.

3. This finding supports Margaret Mead's thesis, made in her opening remarks to the 1978 National Conference on Child Abuse and Neglect, that child abuse represents an excess of concern with the parenting role.

4. National Center on Child Abuse and Neglect, 1977 Analysis of Child Abuse and Neglect Research, op. cit., p. 28.

5. Green, op. cit., p. 18, also notes that the highest percentage of alcoholics was found among the neglectful mothers in his sample.

6. This finding differs somewhat from Kotelchuck, op. cit., p. 16, who found that mothers of abused children had less help with child care.

Chapter VI
SUMMARY AND DISCUSSION

Summary of Findings

This study, carried out between 1975 and 1977, was funded by the National Center on Child Abuse and Neglect in an effort to answer the question: "What are the operative factors or pervasive influences that result in the permanent discontinuation of abusive or neglectful behavior in some parent figures and recidivism in others?" For this purpose, 171 families were interviewed and gave permission for case records to be reviewed. Complaints or suspicions of child abuse or neglect on the part of these families had been reported to protective services departments located in New York, Ohio, Minnesota, Colorado and Tennessee in 1972-73. These departments had served these families for at least several months and in many instances were still active with them at the time of the interview.

The families studied were predominantly female-headed, single-parent families with a median of three children. The typical mother had started childbearing at 19 and was 30 years old at the time of the study. The families were usually living at the poverty level, dependent either on limited earning powers or public funds. Their recent histories were characterized by many forms of stress, particularly marital, and their difficulties were by no means limited to childrearing. Chronic pathology, such as alcoholism or severe depression, was present in a substantial minority, but no one form was predominant. The families tended to be relatively isolated, limiting their contacts to a few members of the extended family and friends but cut off from neighbors and from organizational affiliations.

Health, school, and relationship problems were reported for many of the children in these families. Parental attitudes toward their parenting role were typically mixed, involving some satisfactions as well as consciousness of the responsibilities and the difficulties of childrearing. Their expressions of values in relation to childrearing tended to stress physical care somewhat more strongly than emotional support. The childhood experiences reported ranged from the relatively comfortable to the severely traumatic, but histories of child abuse were not common.

Complaints of neglect were almost twice as common as complaints of abuse. Institutional sources such as agencies were more likely to make complaints than were individuals. For half the sample, the complaints that resulted in the family's inclusion in the study were not the first. Seventy-five percent appeared valid to the research staff; the remainder appeared doubtful. Most families were not involved in court action.

Most families had more than one worker during the period in which the case was active. Typically, one worker--usually female, under the age of 35, with a bachelor's degree and limited experience in protective services--was assigned for a typical period of 16 months during the 2 years that cases were usually active. Families were offered a wide range of conventional social services. The most frequently used service was placement in a foster care setting or with relatives. Children were placed for a median period of 12 months; most had returned home by the time of the interview.

Most families were offered at least one form of service to supplement counseling by the worker and were often given three or more. The analysis indicated that refusal of services was a more common problem than lack of available resources. Services related to material needs, such as medical care, financial aid and housing, were most likely to be used. Refusal rates were highest for parent groups, mental hygiene services, and homemakers. Respondents varied in their assessments of the services given but their overall response to protective services tended to be favorable.

Most families were judged to have shown some improvement in childrearing but improvements in other problem areas were not common. Most indicators of improvement in childrearing suggested better physical care, rather than more subtle psychological changes in attitudes.

The most useful measure of "discontinuation" of abusive or neglectful behavior proved to be an index of improvement consisting of a series of judgments made by research staff. When this measure was related to independent variables describing the families and the service system with which they were involved, it was found that the most influential were the mother's age, her housekeeping ability, her non-authoritarian attitudes, a relatively long period of agency activity, and a moderate number of services in addition to counseling. Mothers under 33 were more likely to improve than older mothers. Families served 2 years or longer were also more likely to show improvement, as were those who received three to four services in addition to counseling. The relationship between housekeeping ability and improvement presents problems of interpretation, as does the relationship with authoritarian attitudes, since there are no base line data to indicate where the parent was located in relation to these measures before service intervention.

The return of children from foster care was associated with family size and adequacy of income. Implications of some of these findings were discussed in Chapter V. Here, we look at some of the broader implications of the study experience, particularly for research and possibly for agency practice and family policy.

Implications for Research and Practice

Few, if any, findings from a single study are conclusive even when the study has the benefit of a relatively large and representative sample, a strong design, skillful data collection, and an imaginative analysis. The problems dealt with in the field of social work are too subject to change for even the most soundly based findings to be certain of relevance for more than half a decade, if that long. Nevertheless, some studies have many of the strengths named and can point directly to policy and practice implications. The findings of others are valuable mainly when they are reviewed together with related studies to show sufficient agreement among the findings to point reasonably clearly in a given direction. Such qualifying terms as "reasonably clearly" are important since it is rare for studies dealing with the same problems to produce results that are totally uncontradictory or unambiguous. The findings of still other studies are mainly valuable for the education they provide the investigators that can result in plans for stronger and more definitive studies, when and if continuity of funding is possible. This study qualifies for the latter two categories.

The Importance of Longitudinal Research

The findings of this study indicate that a retrospective study may provide some valuable clues for the answers to the questions it poses but it will give definitive answers only on those variables, such as the client's age, that are clearly independent of the outcome variable. More subtle, complex attitudinal variables seem to raise the omnipresent problem of circularity. Did the mother's improved capacity to rear her children without abusing or neglecting them lead her to feel better about herself and free her from depression, which in turn made her a better housekeeper? Or did she first decide to clean her house out of fear of the worker or the desire to make a good impression, which encouraged the worker to be more supportive, thereby enabling the mother to function better in her childrearing role? Did the mother always recognize that children should not be expected to be absolutely obedient and did this relative permissiveness make her more accepting of the help she was given, leading in turn to a more generalized improvement? There is no way to avoid these dilemmas other than through the use of longitudinal designs that provide base line data, defining where the subject is initially and permitting changes to be traced over time. This necessity is clearly recognized in relation to predictive studies whose goal is to determine whether young mothers of infants "at risk" will in fact abuse or neglect their children at some future stage of development. The need, however, is equally strong in studies such as this one, addressed to the question of how such parents change after the abuse/neglect pattern is established.

Another positive feature of longitudinal studies is the greater capacity of the research staff to identify a more representative and less self-selective sample than one that must be identified after the fact. All potential respondents, including clients of protective services agencies, have the right to refuse participation in research. Some will refuse even when payment is offered, accompanied by a full explanation of the study's purpose and reassurance that participation will have no effect on the services given or on the decisions to be made. Selection of the sample early in the period of service may still lead to under-representation of more difficult, intractable, suspicious parents, but the degree of bias involved is not likely to be as great as is the case with the retrospective study, where the number of "escape hatches" for the hostile or indifferent subject is greater. In addition to geographic mobility, a chronic problem in dealing with almost any population (especially one at poverty level not given to leaving forwarding addresses or answering letters), the problems of contact are compounded where there is little or no meaningful contact of clients with current agency staff members. There may be suspicions of the motives behind the study; or refusal can be used as a form of revenge on the agency for what the parents see as indignities heaped upon them. As was apparent in this study, hostility sometimes produces the reverse reaction in that it motivates respondents to be interviewed for the opportunity it affords for ventilation. To determine whether this form of motivation for responding occurs frequently enough to offset the bias created by the respondent who persists in refusing, would require a detailed study in methodology usually beyond the scope of studies concerned with substantive issues. Financial inducements are clearly a requirement for this type of study and with the increasing stringency of confidentiality requirements will probably become standard procedure for most studies involving direct contact with clients.

Another advantage of an antrospective study is that the amount of work required by agency staff in identifying an appropriate sample based on new intake is less than that required for a retrospective study such as this. The pool of cases that needs to be considered is smaller and the work of identification may be spread over a longer period of time. Selection of a sample at intake also gives research staff a larger measure of control over final decisions, which decreases selection errors and ensures a sample whose characteristics match the intent of the studies.

Implications of the Key Findings for Practice

Some of the key findings of this study are reinforced by findings of other recent studies; others are not. Those that are reinforced obviously have stronger policy implications than those that are contradicted by or not consistent with others. Perhaps the most important implications for practice lie in the findings reported by Berkeley Planning Associates in their evaluation of 11 child abuse and neglect demonstration projects. In the Berkeley study, data were collected for 1724 cases of families served by the projects evaluated, located in various parts of the country. Among the outcome measures used was a worker judgment for "reduced propensity for future abuse and neglect." Among the agency variables that influenced this outcome were the use of lay services (Parents Anonymous and lay therapy) and the length of time in treatment. The effects of the first variable could not be assessed in the League study since none of the agencies involved made extensive use of such services at the time the families in the sample were being served.   In relation to the length of time in treatment, the Berkeley report states: "It is apparent that clients who are in treatment a longer period of time do somewhat better in treatment.   Only in Arlington, Arkansas, and Union County are the differences statistically significant but for the whole data set, 14% more of the clients in treatment 6 months or more improved, compared to those in treatment a shorter period of time;   in most projects, the same pattern is seen."[1]

As was indicated in Chapter IV, the League study found that 2 years or more of service was usually necessary before improvement could be seen.   The longer time period may reflect the difference between the pressures placed on conventional protective services and the relative advantages of demonstration projects that usually, although not always, operate under more favorable conditions.   The Berkeley report cites two other studies where period of service was a significant factor in the improvement rate.[2]

The Center for Social Research as Lehigh University followed 328 families cited for child abuse during the period of 1967 to 1976. They reported the effect of the length of service in the opposite direction. "The total number of incidents (of abuse) is positively related to length of service during the initial citation case opening and to the amount of service received before the first citation. The amount of case work is correlated with the number of physical abuse episodes, the number of emotional abuse episodes and the number of neglect episodes...and with placement."[3]   This relationship is to be expected for a protective service agency if its staff consistently assumes an authoritarian role to the exclusion of the more supportive aspects of service. The more episodes of abuse, the more attention given. Studies involving agencies whose policies favor and whose staff practices a combination of support and authority in their approach to parents produce, as the League study did, findings in which length of service does not apparently depend on the number of incidents of abuse observed. Another finding in the Lehigh study is more consistent with both the League and the Berkeley findings: "...The families (of those involved in some form of therapy) in the nonrepetition group had substantially more therapy contacts than had those where there was repetition."[4]

In any case, these findings seem to indicate that parents charged with abuse and neglect are not candidates for brief therapy and that programs must be structured for long-term treatment. Time is apparently the only variable that is reported as significant in more than one study. Neither in the League study nor in the Berkeley study was any measure of the quality of care (size of case load, worker's training, etc.) found to have a direct impact on the outcome for the parent. The Berkeley study found a small relationship between frequency of contact and favorable outcome;[5] the League study found none. On the other hand, the Berkeley study did not find a relationship between the number of services and favorable outcome; the League study did. One can only agree with the conclusion of the Berkeley evaluators that the field's present level of knowledge about effective intervention programs is low, and expectations for success can be no higher than the 40% to 50% indicated by the Berkeley study.[6] The relatively high proportion of successful outcomes in the League study is apparently due to the self-selection that is inevitable in retrospective studies. Parents do cease to be abusive and neglectful, but just what protective service workers and other professionals in the community can do to increase the rate of improvement, apart from "staying with" the family for a substantial period of time, has yet to be clearly identified.

On another variable, the evidence is ambiguous, but because of its importance it merits attention. In the League study, the younger the mother was at the time of intervention the more likely she was to improve. The age of the mother at the birth of her first child was not significant. In the Berkeley study, the age of the mother was not a significant variable. The Lehigh study reported, however, "a significant negative correlation ..between the age of the mother at the time of the child's birth and subsequent physical abuse of the child...Younger mothers were more likely to have children who were later abused or grossly neglected."[7] Both the League and the Lehigh studies were carried out in response to the same question posed by the funding agency, but the differences in the populations involved, the time span covered, the range of agencies, differences in the method of data collection, in analysis, and in the outcome variables make it difficult, if not impossible, to explain the differences in findings. Nevertheless, it is important to note these inconsistencies since they have implications not necessarily perceived by those in research. Reports from the field suggest a growing concern that teen-age unwed mothers, whose numbers have increased in recent years, may have greater potential for child abuse than older mothers. In some quarters, this belief can become a justification for a return to what is now seen as an outdated agency policy: the preference for adoption as the optimal solution for the problems of the unwed mother. It is possible that the findings noted are not really contradictory; the younger mother may be more likely to be involved in more incidents of abuse but also more likely to be responsive to treatment. Both findings help make the case for early intervention but in the form of more and better inhome services, not necessarily those involving separation of mother and child.

Needed Research

The conclusion of the first cycle of research funding by the National Center on Child Abuse and Neglect will elicit many opinions as to what types of research are needed and which should be given priority. Early reviews indicate that dissatisfaction with the "state of the art" is still prevalent. Monica Holmes's assessment is typical: "Based on our rather exhaustive review of the literature, we concluded that the research in this area suffers from lack of definitional clarity and from exceptionally poor methodology."[8]   Thomas, the editor of the Human Ecology Forum, in an introduction to a review of current research, states:

> Child abuse research over the last 15 years has been sketchy. The number of cases studied by any one researcher has tended to be quite small, definitions of abuse and neglect have varied from study to study, and the period of time abusing families have been studied has been brief. Most scholars agree that comprehensive research needs to be conducted. Larger samples are needed; studies should follow families over a number of years; new research should proceed from a common set of definitions and protocols. If research is developed in conjunction with helping programs, the program model should also be duplicated in numerous sites around the country. Finally, attempts should be made to include families from all levels of society to overcome an earlier bias of studying only families of lower socioeconomic status.[9]

Simpkins, in her review of the first-round NCCAN-funded research, writes: "All of these things (subject population, operational definitions, problems of data gathering, comparison groups, etc.) have proven so problematic for the retrospective ACYF studies that most findings will be judged as suspect due to factors of validity, as difficult or impossible to interpret due to ambiguities inherent in the method or as of such limited generalizability that they do not apply to the appropriate subjects."[10]

The 1977 Analysis of Child Abuse and Neglect Research reports major problems in virtually every category it surveys. Research on the definition of child abuse and neglect, for instance, is limited; even "current estimates of incidence vary so widely as to minimize any confidence that may be placed in them."[11]

A broad range of studies has been carried out on what the report calls the "psychosocial ecology" of child abuse and neglect. The report notes that "through these studies a few tentative steps have been taken to describe the interdependent nature of these various forces as they affect the potential for abuse and neglect. The major gap is the lack of research on the relations of social institutional forces to child abuse and neglect. The gap not only affects the study of the psychosocial ecology of child abuse and neglect but also that of prevention and treatment."[12]

In its chapter on studies of prevention and treatment, the report notes that "one of the major difficulties in assessing the efficacy of different programs is the lack of standard means of measurement." In most programs, "changes are measured by the rate of recurrence of abuse." Some of the limitations of the use of this outcome variable were discussed in Chapter IV. The report concludes that "overall research has provided little comparability of findings among programs, thus making it difficult to assess under what conditions treatment methods are effective."[13]

These assessments are obviously discouraging for the researcher and the practitioner, all the more so if one recalls that the proposal for this study began, as did others, with a review of the literature that pointed out the inadequacies and uncertainties of the state of knowledge at that time. Yet students of social problems are aware that the development of a body of knowledge based on systematic research that complements the empirical knowledge of the practitioner is a matter of decades, not 2 or 3 years. What then can reasonably be expected from research efforts in relation to a problem that in our time dates basically from Kempe's identification in the early 1960s of the "battered child syndrome"? In a pattern typical for the social work field, "practice wisdom" has often been based on a handful of clinical studies in which generalizations about the personalities of the parents, such as the role reversal theory, are quoted and requoted until they take on the appearance of scientifically verified fact. The same is true for such explanations of the "causes" of child abuse as the intergenerational effect, i.e., the abusing parent was himself an abused child, has no positive role models, and knows no other way of rearing children. The principal achievement of the current phase of research effort may well be the "demythologizing" of at least some of the assumptions of the last decade, but they have not yet been replaced by findings substantial enough to be considered fact. The period of "demythologizing" may make the student of the problem feel even less knowledgeable and more frustrated than before, but this process is a necessary evil, serving the function of "clearing the decks" and creating a pressure to fill the vacuum with newer and, it is hoped, more soundly based hypotheses to be tested under better conditions than has been true in the past.

If this is the case and if, in fact, the power of the mythology of the field is diminishing, what research now is needed?

Better Typologies. As was indicated in Chapter V, many students of the problem of child abuse and neglect have noted differences in the personality patterns of parents who are abusive and those who are neglectful. Some research efforts, including this League study and those cited in Chapter V, have contributed to the evidence for these differences. Some students of the problem have, at least by implication, questioned this distinction by discussing both categories together, and students have done so by replacing "abuse and neglect" with the term "child maltreatment." From the standpoint of those whose chief concern is social policy, this shift in terminology may be justified, since both child abuse and neglect are forms of failure to carry out adequately the social requirements of the parenting role. For those interested in findings that help determine the best ways of developing better support systems for the family, the specific form that "maltreatment" takes in individual cases may not be a central question. However, for those concerned with understanding the psychosocial dynamics involved and with programs for treatment, whether or not child abuse and child neglect are basically different phenomena is a central question; if they are, in effect, different "diseases," they probably require different modes of treatment. Simpkins, in her review of the NCCAN studies, states that "there is no really appropriate way to interpret findings based on a subject population that is undifferentiated as to neglect or abuse. Certainly no retrospective studies funded in the future should fail to make this distinction."[14] She also recommends that "any research attempting to clarify factors contributing to abuse and neglect should use methodologies adequate to tease out interrelationships. Designs based on the assumption that there is one set of factors contributing to neglect or abuse are not nearly as powerful for identifying contributing factors as are designs searching out typologies. Treatment programs are greatly in need of descriptive typologies in order to carefully design intervention programs."[15]

It is this need for better typologies that perhaps identifies the needed research of highest priority. The fact that concern for abused and neglected children was triggered by a particular form of seriously deviant adult behavior--severe physical battering of young children-- does not mean that the concern must remain focused there in order to deal with the larger problem; the League has maintained that severe battering is the "tip of the iceberg" of a much larger problem.[16] Nor does it mean that differentiation of the "abuse case" from the "neglect case" is the only form of typology available, although some discussants seem to assume that this is the case. It is, in fact, as many investigators have begun to appreciate, an overly simplistic typology. Closer attention to the problem has made many practitioners aware in recent years of, for example, sexual abuse, a form of abuse that is inherently different from the others; the sexually abusive parent may never be physically abusive or necessarily neglectful of the usual requirements of childrearing. And the child's response is not the same as it is to physical abuse or neglect. Whether more consideration needs to be given to emotional neglect is a major problem. Some children, particularly middle and upper class children, may receive a high level of physical care and may never be punished physically, but may have their emotional needs entirely neglected. The inclusion of the emotionally neglected in the legal definition of abuse and neglect--which in turn makes it part of any potential typology--is particularly problematic because, more than other forms of neglect, it opens up the possibility of including in the target population almost every type of childrearing problem and rendering intervention programs unmanageable or meaningless.

Not only is the abuse/neglect typology too simple, but studies using predictive instruments have demonstrated the likelihood of too many false negatives--parents identified as nonabusing who actually are--and false positives--those classed as abusive who actually are not. Kotelchuck discusses the problem in his report of a study of pediatric social illness that included abuse, neglect, failure to thrive, accidents and ingestions--conditions that, in his words, result primarily "from the child's physical and social interaction with his environment and are distinguishable from illness with a more primary congenital or biomedical basis." Kotelchuck notes that within this group, there are many ambiguities. "Many accidents have parental concomitants and many of the child abuse cases have strong accidental characteristics. Thus while the diagnoses of accidental abuse seem distinct, the underlying reality is much less clear."[17] Ceresnie and Starr note in their child abuse study that "...we have the major problem of the lack of any readily apparent complex of characteristics to identify abusive or potentially abusive parents. Results of discriminant function analysis indicate that high percentages of both false positive and false negative classifications would occur from the use of even the best set of differentiating variables. This finding raises a multitude of issues concerning the effects of labeling--whether correct or incorrect--in the design of treatment programs for potentially abusive parents, the potential for the abuse of power in coercing treatment, and so forth."[18]

Some observers have argued that where neglect is concerned, the phenomenon tends to be general, i.e., the child who is not adequately fed or clothed is also likely to be medically and educationally neglected, with perhaps the exception of religious sects that may have deviant ideas of adequate medical care. As was noted in Chapter III, most of the neglect cases in the study were of this generalized nature; cases focused on educational or medical neglect were uncommon. In any case, the current pattern of dichotomizing the problem into abuse and neglect and then overstressing the former does not seem a fruitful approach and should be replaced.

Neglecting the Neglected. As was noted in Chapter IV, all estimates of the incidence of abuse and neglect agree that neglect cases substantially outnumber abuse cases, although ratios may vary from 3 to 1 to 10 to 1. Despite this, many observers have been struck by the fact that both practitioners and researchers focus much more heavily on the abused child than on the neglected. In the case of the earlier clinical studies, originating in medical settings, this focus was understandable. The recent period of heightened attention to the problem began with observation by radiologists of X rays showing old injuries and other trauma not adequately accounted for by parents' stories of accidents. Continuing public discussion and passage of the Child Abuse and Neglect Prevention Act made concerned professionals aware that the cases of battered children reported in the newspapers represented the "tip of the iceberg" covering many situations not as extreme or as life-threatening but nevertheless representing a problem of considerable magnitude. Yet the preoccupation with abuse continues, even when it runs counter to the intent of those concerned. In 3 years of nearly full-time involvement with the child abuse and neglect phenomenon, this investigator has watched repeatedly while discussions ostensibly dealing with both problems increasingly narrowed in focus and dealt only with abuse. In his Profile of Neglect, Polansky reported that when he wrote colleagues to inquire about stimulating new programs of work on child neglect, a surprising number offered descriptions of programs dealing with abuse.[19] This phenomenon was also evident at the 1978 Annual Conference on Child Abuse and Neglect when discussion during a workshop specifically directed to the problem of neglect shifted to abuse-related questions and remained focused on abuse, while none of the participants appeared aware of the shift or drew audience attention to it.

The situation with regard to research is well illustrated by the fact that Polansky is the one investigator who continues to concern himself solely with the problem of neglect, and remains the sole expert despite the expansion of research expertise resulting from NCCAN funding. In fact, if it were not for the concern of an investigator of Polansky's stature in the field, it is difficult to see how the problem of neglect would receive any attention at all.

There are several possible explanations for this phenomenon. Polansky himself notes that "abuse is by no means a univocal phenomenon, but it permits more concise definition than does neglect. The traditional preference of investigators for readily manageable problems may well be a major reason why abuse has been the more popular object of study."[20] In a more recent paper he writes, "Abuse is the more dramatic phenomenon; it can be specified and identified. While neglect may also prove lethal, it is typically insidious, chronic, and terribly private."[21] To these explanations one can add the observation that the abused child is the object of the physician's concern, which ipso facto attracts more attention. Despite the erosion in recent years of the social prestige conferred on the medical profession, it still has the power to attract attention from the media and from the government, and with it funds for new programs that, in turn, generate even more attention to the problem of abuse. The neglected child is more likely to be visible to social workers and teachers, whose powers and resources are considerably more limited.

The abused child presents a universally appealing image to the general public. In an era of political conservatism, inhospitable to the use of large sums of money to meet social needs, the abused child in the 1970s occupies something of the same position as the crippled child of the 1930s. The abused child is a victim, universally seen as helpless and unable to act on his own behalf. Even the most committed believers in private initiative, free enterprise, and the nonintervention of government into family affairs cannot see the abused child as anything other than a victim. It is little wonder that the Child Abuse and Neglect Prevention Act was one of the few pieces of significant social legislation passed in the 1970s.

Finally, one may note that child abuse is a form of violence. It is now a commonplace observation that concern with and interest in violence is an obsession of contemporary American society.

The development of typology does not in itself establish the causes of abuse and neglect but can supply substantial evidence as to where the roots of the problem lie. The concept of "cause" as it is used in relation to this problem is a dubious one. Most discussions are based on the medical model, which assumes that abuse and neglect are diseases for which treatment may be found if the causes are identified. Whether this is the most productive approach for the psychosocial phenomena involved in child abuse and neglect is debatable.

If it is difficult to maintain a simple dichotomy between abuse and neglect, it will be much more difficult to attempt the development of and gain acceptance for a complex typology that reflects more accurately the reality of child maltreatment in American family life than has been the case to date.

Simpkins in her review notes that few attempts have been made so far and adds that "interest in developing typologies as a less simplistic way of approaching etiology has not been high."[22] The reasons for this are probably much the same as those denoting overconcern with the abused child. In addition, however, one must note that the problem is perpetuated by the funding process itself. If studies of abuse are funded, studies of abuse are produced. There is little incentive to break away from the simplistic medical model unless the funding sources are willing to lead the way. An improved framework and new priorities for research in this field are imperative. The suggestions that follow represent two possibilities; there may well be others.

Possible Research Designs to Develop Adequate Typologies. An adequately developed typology would require a large sample of families with children under 16. Data would be collected to include demographic characteristics, socioeconomic descriptors such as those described in the urban version of Polansky's Childhood Level of Living,[24] childrearing methods, parental experiences of childhood, life style, measures of self-esteem, etc. The recently completed studies of child abuse and neglect, particularly those using comparison groups of nonabusing or nonneglecting populations, have yielded findings on a number of variables that apparently differentiate the maltreating parents from others and could be introduced in instruments used in future studies.

Ideally such a sample would be based on census tracts reflecting low, middle, and upper income communities. If large enough, such a sample should include a substantial minority in which some form of abuse or neglect appears. If carried out in states that permit access to registry records on the part of research organizations, the sample can be checked against the records to identify those families who may have been actually reported as abusive or neglectful.

It should be possible to differentiate between clearly reportable cases of abuse and neglect, the marginal groups where neither form of behavior may be frequent or severe, and those families where there is no evidence of abuse or neglect. On the basis of the present evidence, it is likely that the nature of the parent's maltreatment will be among the discriminating variables but other variables may be equally powerful. The result should be a typology that describes several categories associated with social and personality descriptors that should not only add to our understanding but indicate different approaches to intervention.

Another approach, more flawed from a research standpoint but perhaps more practical, would view the populations served by protective service agencies as families who have failed or are in danger of failing in their childrearing role. Again, a large sample of cases from public agencies where the state laws permit direct access to records by research organizations, and whose recording practices are adequate could be reviewed and data extracted from records covering, to the extent feasible, the same kinds of variable that would be obtained in a community survey. Such a study has the obvious disadvantages of sampling from the reported population of abusers/neglecters, not from a community cross-section; of not including the families whose behavior is less visible and escapes reporting; and of having an overrepresentation of the lowest socioeconomic level of the general population. Data from records, although superior for some variables, are not reliable for others. Nevertheless, ample justification remains for such a study for a variety of reasons. Even if poverty does not account wholly for the phenomenon of abuse and neglect, the poor are more vulnerable both to failures in childrearing and to having their failures reported publicly. They are also the most in need of a variety of services that represent a heavy public investment. As was noted in this study, involvement with protective service agencies is not limited to families where abuse or neglect is clearly evident but includes those characterized in this study as "marginal." Differences between this group and those where the evidence of abuse or neglect is more convincing should be particularly instructive. Furthermore, protective service agencies are usually departments of public agencies where other departments may serve populations of a similar socioeconomic level, not charged with abuse or neglect, who may also serve as comparison groups.

A Final Comment

One of the questions--perhaps the key question--posed by students of the problem of child abuse and neglect, implicit in much of what has been said, is whether the problem is a product of certain personality disorders or a social problem that, like so many others, is mainly a derivative of poverty. It may be clear to the reader by now that this investigator is skeptical about the possibility of identifying the abusing or neglecting parents as a distinct diagnostic group and doubts that this is a fruitful approach for research. The role of poverty as a predisposing condition seems to be supported by stronger evidence, as in the recently completed study by the Rutgers University School of Social Work.[23] A review of the items in Polansky's Urban Childhood Level of Living Scale reveals that half require some expenditure of funds, even if only in the form of small sums for carfare or simple toys.[24] Yet, even if poverty is clearly a predisposing condition for child neglect and possibly child abuse as well, it is not sufficient explanation. As has been pointed out in many discussions, most of the poor, even the extremely poor, do not abuse or neglect their children. There must be other variables--whether they involve psychic stress, personality disorders, differences in childrearing practices, assumptions about the nature of parenting or the absence of any theories of childrearing--that explain why some parents are abusive or neglectful and others not. Just what these are we seem to be a long way from knowing.

It is possible that the effort to develop a typology, or any new approach, may not be any more productive than the studies based on the assumption that child abuse reflects a personality disorder. If this happens, it does not necessarily mean that funds and researchers' time have been wasted. Negative findings are sometimes as instructive as positive findings, as was said earlier, if not more so. If we cannot, after much effort, establish a clear explanatory pattern for the phenomenon of child abuse and neglect, it may mean that the maltreatment of children reflects an inherent defect in the structure of our society, that it may be found anywhere because this is a society that does relatively little to support parents in their efforts to fulfill their obligations. If it is more prevalent among the poor, it is because this group has the least support in other life areas as well.

In 1975, Kamerman noted that, except for Canada, no other country, of eight involved in a cross-national study of social services, had found it necessary to develop special programs for identifying abused and neglected children. The existence of the problem is not denied, but in these countries universal maternal and child health programs make it possible to identify and treat abused or neglected children as the need arises without differentiating them and their parents from others. She raises the question: "Can this current stress on child abuse be a "stalking horse"--a way of taking the lead and taking initiative in a movement to expand resources and provision for child welfare programs generally?"[26] The principal value of current research and demonstration efforts in child abuse and neglect may well lie in what we learn about the nature of our society's relationship to the task of rearing children. If current research and demonstrations, of which the League study is one part, lead to a broader support system for families, they will have been well worth the investment of funds and effort, even if they do not answer to anyone's great satisfaction the questions that were raised at their beginning.

References

1.   Berkeley Planning Associates, Evaluation of Child Abuse and Neglect Demonstration Projects, 1974-77, Vol. III Adult Client. National Center for Health Services Research, December, 1977, p. 86.

2.   Berkeley Planning Associates, op. cit., p. 89.

3.   Herrenkohl, Roy. Summary: An Investigation of the Effects of a Multidimensional Service Program in Recidivism/Discontinuation of Child Abuse and Neglect, Center for Social Research, Lehigh University (photocopy), June, 1978.

4.   Herrenkohl, ibid., p. 16.

5.   Berkeley Planning Associates, op. cit., pp. 99-101.

6.   Berkeley Planning Associates, op. cit., iv.

7.   Herrenkohl, op. cit., pp. 11-12.

8.   Community Council of Greater New York. Improving Services to Families in Brooklyn: Joint Strategies for the Child Protective Services and Mental Health Systems, Proceedings of a Research Utilization Workshop (mimeo) New York, April, 1978. p. 2.

9.   Hanna, Thomas. The Human Ecology Forum, Vol. 8, No. 4, Spring, 1978, p. 6.

10. Simpkins, Celeste. Report on Child Abuse and Neglect Research, (draft), August, 1978, p. 54.

11. National Center on Child Abuse and Neglect, op. cit., p. 13.

12. National Center on Child Abuse and Neglect, op. cit., p. 19.

13. National Center on Child Abuse and Neglect, op. cit., p. 26.

14. Simpkins, op. cit., p. 54.

15. Simpkins, op. cit., p. 62.

16. Lunsford, William. Statement Before the Select Committee on Education, U.S. House of Representatives, October, 1973, p. 1.

17. Kotelchuck, Milton. Child Abuse: Prediction and Misclassification. (photocopy), 1977, pp. 2-3.

18. Ceresnie, Steven, and Starr, R.H., Jr. Child Abuse: A Controlled Study of Social and Family Factors, (photocopy), 1977, p. 4.

19. Polansky, Norman; Hally, Carolyn; Polansky, Nancy. Profile of Neglect, U.S. Department of Health, Education, and Welfare, Social and Rehabilitation Service, Community Services Administration, 1975, p. 3.

20. Ibid.

21. Polansky, Norman; Chalmers, Mary Anne; Buttenwieser, Elizabeth and Williams, David. The Father's Role in Child Neglect, (photocopy), 1978, p. 1.

22. Simpkins, op. cit., p. 15.

23. Woloch, Isabel, and Horowitz, Berny, Factors Relating to Levels of Child Care Among Families Receiving Public Assistance in New Jersey, Volume F (photocopy), Research Center, Rutgers Graduate School of Social Work and New Jersey Division of Youth and Family Services, 1977.

24. Polansky, Norman; Chalmers, Mary Anne; Buttenwieser, Eliza-beth, and Williams, David, "Assessing Adequacy of Child Caring: An Urban Scale, Child Welfare, Vol. 47, No. 7, July-August, 1978, pp. 439-449.

25. Polansky et al, op. cit., pp. 443-447.

26. Kamerman, Sheila B. "Cross-National Perspectives on Child Abuse and Neglect," Children Today, Vol. 4, No. 3, May-June, 1975.